FULL CIRCLE

FULL CIRCLE

A True Story

ALI MOHAMMED

Library of Congress Control Number: 2012908808
ISBN: Hardcover   978-1-4771-1294-6
                 Softcover   978-1-4771-1293-9
                 Ebook   978-1-4771-1295-3

To order additional copies of this book, contact:
Xlibris Corporation
0-800-644-6988
www.xlibrispublishing.co.uk
Orders@xlibrispublishing.co.uk
303594

CONTENTS

It all started on Thursday morning of 28 April 1988 when I suddenly heard the sound of heavy machine guns and bombs, and screams of children, women, and men from a small house where I lived.

We all live at the camp, in a small village called Jarso, where we do farming during the day and come back to the camp late in the evening, where we wash, feed, and sleep.

As usual we get up early in the morning before daybreak. As a matter of practice, the first thing we do is routine check-ups and daily maintenance on every single machine.

Each tractor has its attachments. It has to be engaged to the appropriate implements before we proceed to the farm field, which is not far from the camp, about three miles away.

This has been our day-to-day job from ploughing to harvesting according to the schedule supplied by the planning department to cultivate about 3,000 hectares of forest land.

Jarso is a tiny village in the far west corner of Ethiopia, about 200 miles before the Sudanese border, and this part of Ethiopia is very much known for its fertile land and forestry.

A program of re-settlement was introduced by the government to move large number of people from the desert and dry part of northern Ethiopia to the west and south-west part of Ethiopia, which is very fertile.

Portions of settlers are allocated at Jarso and surrounding areas. The entire settlement operations are controlled and regulated by the political cadres of the ruling party.

The settlers are strictly not allowed to go back to their original birthplace. And any illegal movement anywhere is controlled through roadblocks and other means.

*   *   *

Ethiopia lies in the north-eastern part of the horn of Africa between 3⁰N and 15⁰N latitude and 33⁰E and 48⁰E longitudes. The country is landlocked and surrounded by Djibouti to the east, Somalia to the south-east, Kenya to the south, Sudan to the west, and Eritrea to the north and north-east.

Ethiopia has a total area of 1,127,127 square kilometers, and its topographical diversity encompasses high and rugged mountains, flat-topped plateau, and deep gorge with rivers and rolling plains.

Ethiopia was originally called Abyssinia, the oldest state in sub-Saharan Africa. The dynasty descendant of King Menelik, the son of King Solomon and the Queen Sheba and the legacy of Monarchy ended during the removal of Emperor Haile Selassie.

Ethiopia is a unique and distinctive state among the African countries. The ancient monarchy maintained its freedom from the colonial rulers except from 1936-41, owing to the Italian occupation during the Second World War.

On 12 September 1974 Haile Selassie, who had ruled since 1930, was deposed and a socialist state established under a collective military dictatorship called the Derg.

Lt. Col. Mengistu H. Mariam became the head of state in 1977, and during this period, there was a great deal of political, economical, and social unrest not only in Ethiopia, but also the entire region of the Horn of Africa.

Throughout this time and the following years, Ethiopia had been torn apart by the bloody war against Eritrea and Somalia, internal uprisings, wide-scale drought, and the massive refugee problems.

The human factor has also exasperated and worsened the condition of living not only for those who lived in the rural areas, but for a much larger populace across the country. Shortage of food, clean water, and medicine are among a few of the crucial problems faced by the country.

Ethiopia has never recovered from many years of civil war and drought and during this period, the re-settlement program has been introduced as a lasting solution and the mass exodus of people has begun 1985.

The operation was designed by the ruling party and carried out by the political cadres, which are the eyes and ears of the ruling party, very much known for their brutal killings, torture, and rape.

1985 is the year when Ethiopia was hit by the drought severely, creating shortage of food, medicine, and clean water, mounting the death toll to the highest peak.

In a short span of time, the famine that struck the villages caused thousands of deaths due to hunger and diseases, especially among those who lived in deep rural areas and out of reach of any assistance.

*   *   *

In 1980 I completed the national metric exam. I later joined the technical college and studied agro-mechanics technology—the skill that is required for operation, maintenance, and repair of farm machineries.

After I graduated in 1984, I got employment at the Ministry of Agriculture as a mechanic for farm machineries in the central region of Ethiopia, relatively fertile and peaceful.

Few months later, I transferred to the remote western part of Ethiopia, at the settlement areas in Assossa region. I was among other employees who had been called to be part of the Agricultural Mechanisation Service Corporation (AMSC), who operates under the Ministry of Agriculture.

The old town of Assossa is found at the far western part of Ethiopia, about five hundred miles away from the capital, which is about fifty miles before the borderline of the Sudan to the north.

At the beginning of March 1986 we began our first journey from Addis at the peak of the hot season. We drove through the bushes and dusty roads to the very old town of Assossa.

Assossa is the regional coordination centre for the settlement program. On our arrival, we were notified by the political cadres who were in charge and command of any activity in the settlement area.

The political cadres are carefully recruited to serve and prolong the ruling military junta, purposely to create confusion and havoc among the nation. They are responsible for the killings of thousands of innocent people.

A week later, most of us had been assigned and dispersed to different sites of the settlements areas. I was allocated about ten miles to the south of Assossa, a tiny farm village called Megelle.

Megelle was a newly formed settler's village. It was late in the afternoon when I arrived at Megele. The new settlers were arriving in different kinds of vehicles busses, trucks, and many activities on their arrival. It was dark and raining.

A large number of people crowded on the open fields; they had come from very far, from the northern part of the country, many of them trapped in the rain and cold with no shelter or food.

Most of the settlers were very sick, vomiting and unable to move; people were dying by the minute and buried on the spot. At the same time, concerns were growing about the sharp rise in the death toll and the outbreaks of deadly diseases.

The effect of the drought and the war brought millions to starvation and death. Ethiopia depends heavily on agriculture, which is often affected by drought.

The government began to move hundreds of thousands of people away from the dry desert land from the north to the fertile land at the south-west in an attempt to provide a lasting solution to food shortages.

When I found myself in the middle of these chaotic activities, emotionally I was shocked and devastated. I was witnessing the worst human tragedy, and it was the most traumatic experience of my life.

It was very visible; anyone could observe the magnitude of the catastrophe and the severity caused by the drought, overwhelming and bizarre beyond imagination. The sanitation and the living condition in general worsened as more and more people arrived by the day.

As a civil servant, I had a commitment—to serve the settlers to farm the land to save life. Those who had died were gone, and we had to save the living—that was our focus, our objective.

There was shortage of basic and fundamental necessities—food, shelter, and medicines, which could have saved many lives. The children were among the ones who were affected the most.

The government and international aid agencies were directing their efforts to the rescue mission. The Irish concern int'l (non-governmental organization) was the first to arrive for the supplying of food, clean water, and medicine in Assossa and the surrounding settlement areas.

Within one week we organized ourselves in one corner of the village and began clearing the forest, preparing the land for the farm operation, which was about two miles away from the village.

The pressure was mounting from every side that we start our operation. A couple of weeks later, we began the farming operation with eight Russian-made tractors, about two thousand hectares of land.

At the start of the operation, there was no specific time for break or change of shift. We worked fourteen hours a day, every one of us willing to work long hours due to the circumstances.

We did not have a camp or shelter where we came to rest—just the open field, in the middle of the forest. Everything was so fast, and there was no time to think for our basic needs.

During the first few weeks, we slept on the open space surrounded by tractors. A few of us would go for hunting small wild animals, and that was our main source of food as there was no other option.

And before long everything started to take shape. Many temporary houses had been built and the settlers accommodated in different shelters. And we become more and more aware of the surroundings of Megelle, the new farm village.

Mr Tesfaye was the unit manager in charge of the operation, and among the workers were the tractor operators, mechanics, and surveyors—all together about twenty-eight of us allocated for the site.

In those circumstances when a human tragedy occurred we felt obliged to push aside our personal interest and react towards the disaster as a moral obligation. And that was exactly what happened.

Our priority was to save human lives and provide sustainable food supply. We had to work very hard to feed the settlers. A good harvest for the coming season was the bottom line.

Before the start of the rainy season, we managed to cultivate two thousand hectares of land according to the schedule. This was encouraging and a sign of good hope.

*   *   *

In mid 1987, I have been offered a short-term course in East Germany sponsored and organised by one of the biggest suppliers of farm machineries based in Germany, Fortscritt land machinen.

The team made up of six employees from different farm locations to upgrade our knowledge of modern farm machineries. For us it was a break to get away for a while.

One afternoon we boarded the flight at Bole International in Addis, and just over midnight, we landed in Berlin, the German capital. There were two people waiting for us at Berlin Airport—the school principal and the driver Mr Ralph.

We drove through the night. The small van was packed with meals and beverages. After a long journey, at about mid-morning, we arrived at a small town called Bad Frankenhausen.

We had a short sleep at the guesthouse that was provided for us. Late in the afternoon, the school governing body conveyed to us the school schedule and programs until the completion of our study.

It was a technical school. It provided technical knowledge of various kinds of skills for German and foreign students. Probably, it was one of the oldest schools. It had many departments mainly based on practical lessons, specifically on advanced farm machineries.

Throughout our stay and during every weekend, there was a special arrangement for us to tour historical places in East Germany. We were introduced to big plants, mega factories, and manufacturers of advanced farm machineries.

There was also a program for us apart from attending the school—to go and witness some of the Nazi concentration camps, museums, and collections from the past.

We visited some of the concentration camps. During our tour through the camp and inside the buildings, the German lady who was guiding us explained in detail the horrific incidents in different spots within the camp, which took place several decades ago.

Sometimes I felt uneasiness and became distressed during and after visiting the concentration camps—the places where gruesome killings took place. Beside the sliding pictures and museums, the physical buildings and the material it contained are clear evidence.

Whenever I visit such places, I felt something inexplicable. Most of us remained silent and numb with deep sadness; the sad and horrifying thoughts about the place remained in our mind for long time.

*   *   *

After three months of training, we returned to Ethiopia and reported to our head office in Addis, and a few days later, we went back to our locations, Assossa, the regional coordination center.

A couple of weeks after my arrival in Assossa, I was transferred to a new site called 'Sirba 1'(a tiny specific site, where our camp was built) in Jarso area deep in the forest and far from the towns or villages, far from everything.

Mr Eshetu Mulat, the head of regional coordination centre, has given us a brief about the farming operation and other related matters, but nothing of the security issue at Jarso.

Jarso was the remotest area located about a hundred miles away south of Assossa, and 'Sirba 1' was a new farm site, and none of us had been there previously. At the time, I had no idea how Jarso looked like.

There had been many speculations about the security problems at Jarso, that it was a high-risk security region, the threat of kidnappings, the resistance fighters, and so on and so forth. I heard many bad things.

In mid of January 1988, we arrived specifically at a place called 'Sirba 1', among the newly formed very tiny dusty settlers' village, located in Jarso in the middle of a forest. The forest covered a large area, stretching out hundreds of miles across the Sudanese border.

The first thing that came to my mind was to adjust myself with the new environment and forget all about city life to be able to participate among the workers and perform whatever was required of me.

We were in total about forty workers at 'Sirba 1' camp in different job categories—tractor operators, mechanics, store men, etc.; some of them lived with their wife and kids.

The Sirba 1 camp was newly built. The workers' house, the store, and everything looked identical. Built from corrugated sheet metal, it was more likely a temporary accommodation.

I walked down slowly through the middle of the camp guided by one of our workers to the small house allocated for me. As we got closer, he pointed out the house, where I should be staying before he returned.

I opened the door wide. The room was completely dark and empty. There was nothing to sit on or lie down. I was hungry, thirsty, and exhausted; however, I was expecting and mentally prepared for such an environment.

I lit my candles and spread my beddings on the floor and took out my diary. As a hobby I wrote down the events from my daily life for my personal memory. Soon I was gone, fast asleep, and it was my first night at Sirba 1, Jarso.

I got up early in the morning and went outside. The camp was surrounded by thick and green forest. It was a beautiful day, and I toured through the camp, introducing myself to everyone.

Jarso was very remote and communication was possible only by means of two-way VHF radio transmitter, which can get to every corner of the country. At the center of the camp were the kitchen and the dining hall, facing each other.

Late in the evening, we held our first meeting among the workers. We discussed several issues related to our operation and got an opportunity to get to know each other. It was more of a friendly meeting and nothing of the security issues had been discussed.

It was time for ploughing; there was no time to spare. Before the beginning of the rainy season, we had to plough day and night—three shifts of eight hours' duration.

Everything was running smoothly according to the plan. Our primary objective was ploughing, and it had to be completed before the beginning of the rainy season, end of May 1988.

Farming requires teamwork, and people needed to have self-motivation, encouragement, and high spirits and morale. Good communication was also very important. However, the interests of the workers have to be maintained in order to achieve good performance.

Every one of us was determined to bring about change through good performance and high productivity. I had to take part in every activity in the camp as well as on the field. According to the circumstances, one had to change the way of thinking and deeds in administration and other areas.

At the time, I had little or no experience of the administrative work. I was mainly on the technical side, but I needed to learn and be part of them to gain more experience and get to know everyone.

I learnt to adapt myself with the environment, the settlers, and the job very quickly. Everything looked promising, and our daily output was increasing ahead of the schedule.

As we engaged in the farming activities and run smoothly something unexpected to happen, which was in our thought, but our focus was in our daily operations and that made us less concerned about our security, which changed our life forever.

As a matter of practice, every morning the operators drove away with their tractors and the rest of the workers transported from and to the farm by the service pickup car. This was how it was been done seven days a week since the beginning.

14 April 1988—the beginning of a critical chain of events, which lasted for many years and the primary reason why I am here today. My story displays how the effect of a single incident has the power to change everything.

THE BEGINNING OF EVERYTHING

Day One

Thursday morning, 14 April 1988. At about seven thirty, I came back from the farm and went to my house. Usually, I had my breakfast in my small house before I proceeded on any maintenance work at the workshop.

It was a beautiful day bright sky Thursday morning. The rest of the workers who remained at the camp were completely unaware of the danger about to happen in a short space of time.

While sitting in my room having my breakfast, I heard a big bang followed by the sound of light and heavy weapons, getting louder and louder by the second.

Machine guns, mortar launchers, and the screaming of children, women, and men, many kinds of noises turned the peaceful morning quickly into a chaotic one.

At the beginning, I was very shocked and nervous. I never moved from my bed where I was sitting. The storm of bullets flying in every direction was so horrifying and frightening that it is difficult to describe.

I remained in bed for a while without making any effort to move or hide, as there was no time or space to run or hide. Constantly, the bullets were penetrating the wall of corrugated sheet metal. It was a nerve wrecking moment.

It happened suddenly and unexpectedly. At first I panicked and was terrified, but in order to survive I had to follow the survival methods, force myself to calm down and think properly to save myself.

I thought about the rumors we had heard long before we came to Jarso. The security issue, about which we were never concerned about, had now become real and regrettably too late to think about the past.

The first time in my life, I felt that I was in real trouble and that my life was in real danger, trapped in a small room nowhere to go. Soon I noticed the movement of heavily armed people through the window.

Ever since I was a child, I would get up early in the morning, and the first thing I would do was to open my window wide to get fresh air, but what I got that morning was different—the rebel fighters.

I could hear orders being given in loud voices, as they ran cautiously up and down, from side to side, most of them young men and women, very alert and vigilant.

They looked furious and nervous. Most of the men were bare bodied, wearing a kind of scarf over their head and the chain of ammunitions across their chests shining and visible from where I stood.

They appeared to be rebel fighters, resistance forces against the government. And they came from very far, deep in the forest, most probably outside of the Ethiopian territory, from Sudan.

The one thing bothering me was how I could make myself available. In that circumstance, it would be very hard to imagine or even to think what would happen within the next minute.

I had many kinds of concerns—they might throw a bomb in my room or burn the house as I was sitting or spread a rain of bullets. It was the scariest and the most agonising moment as there was no chance to escape.

Soon after, the storm of bullets slowed down. Very slowly, I got up to my feet from the wooden bed where I was sitting. In order to get a clear view, I moved slowly closer to the side of the open window.

I discovered they took control of the entire camp and were busy searching one house after another forcing the workers out of their rooms. I could hear the sounds of female fighters swearing and shouting from not very far away.

I noticed some of our workers who remained at the camp being dragged out of their rooms at gunpoint, badly beaten with sticks and forced to lie down on the ground next to the main entrance on the open space.

I was waiting for my turn. I have decided to stay where I was sitting and they should come and get me, if I got out of the house, there was a great possibility I could be shot, If I remained in my room, the one thing bothering me was the raging of fire.

I could be burnt alive. Everywhere everything was on fire. Soon I noticed one of the fighters coming towards the room where I was sitting. And the more he got closer, my heart started pounding faster and faster. I thought that was it.

Nervously and cautiously he came closer. I could see him clearly through the open window, but I was not very sure if he could see me from outside, as it was shadowy and unclear. At that moment, I panicked and struggled to calm myself down.

When he was about ten feet away from where I stood, he stopped and started to aim and simultaneously shout, Is there anyone in this house?

I quickly replied, 'Yes, I'm here.'

He said, 'Put both of your hands over your head and come out slowly.' I did as he said. I could see his fingers on the trigger, on high alert, and suspiciously he came closer.

I knew if I made a wrong move, it could easily cost my life. As I came out slowly, he said in a loud voice, 'Turn your face against the wall.' I turned my back quickly as he said that.

He came closer and searched me before he kicked me on my lower back. He then told me to join the rest of my colleagues who had already been there lying on the ground next to the main entrance.

The last ten minutes were very agonizing. It was a moment of tense emotions, because of the wide spread speculations about the brutality of the kidnapers for no reason, but I was still alive and breathing. That was the beginning of a new chapter.

As I walked down slowly to the main gate, I realized the entire camp was in flames, from corner to corner. The workers' house, offices, the workshop, and everything was burning.

Our main store contained highly flammable materials, spare parts, engine oils, tyres, and food items, and the combination created one big storm of fire rising to the sky. It was very scary.

My lower back was still in pain, but that did not bother me at all. Slowly, I went and mixed with my colleagues who were still in pain and shock surrounded by heavily armed men and women rebel fighters.

Five of us were sitting close to each other—the store keeper Haile and three junior mechanics Gecho, Feisal, and Tolossa, and myself—all of us between the ages of twenty and twenty-seven.

Slowly we start to whisper to each other who these people were. Where did they come from? What did they want? Many questions, but none of us got the answer.

During the invasion, most of the workers already had gone to the field early in the morning and could not be reached. Few of them who remained at the camp escaped to the forest through the fence, unnoticed.

Five of us whispered, 'We have to obey and accept any of their orders without resistance or confrontation. We have to avoid any tragedy in order to save our lives.'

It was the beginning of new chapter, new phenomenon, we have to be strong and prepare ourselves mentally as well as physically for the worst. It was difficult even to imagine what lay ahead.

Within a short space of time everything had changed completely. Suddenly we became prisoners, over which we had no control over, and we had no idea what they would do next.

A short while later, a sound came through, 'getup', followed by intimidations. We then quickly got to our feet. When I stood up, I saw my small house was in flames, burning out of control.

I was deeply saddened my house, where I lived peacefully for the last four months, the pictures of my families hanging on the wall, my personal items, and everything in it was burning.

For a while I felt angry. I hated them, but there was nothing I could have done. There was no time to express my feelings. I kept my thought to myself and quickly shifted my thinking towards the next move.

Close to our camp there was another camp belongs to the Irish concern org. who provide a great deal of assistance to the settler in terms of food medical care and shelter.

They have saved thousands of life, especially those of children and the sick and vulnerable. The Irish Concern Org. regarded as the backbone of the operation in the re-settlement areas.

The two young women who co-ordinate and ran this project, whom I knew by their first name, Fiona from and Marry from Ireland, also took part in conservation programs.

On many occasions, I met with them and shared ideas about the overall operations. They ran their own programs independently without any interference by the political cadres or anyone else.

At the center of their camp, a very large and big tent was visible, which contained large amounts of food substance, blankets, construction materials, and so many items donated from Europe for the feeding program of the settlers.

I could hear the burning sound of materials, including their living house and a number of motor vehicles standing on raw and ready for Thursday morning service.

One of the rebels said, 'One line, queue in one line.' We lined up as he said. It was a tense and nervous moment. They wanted to vacate the area very quickly. They knew the army was not far away.

Whenever they gave us orders it was always followed by intimidation and yelling, intentionally to get us panicked and confused and to drive us out of the area very quickly.

Soon all of us were dragged out of the camp, disrespectfully, through the main gate. They deliberately kicked us to embarrass us and to show us they were the ones in charge of everything.

As we emerged outside of the camp, we saw four men escorted by two rebel fighters. The four men were among the settlers who arrived recently through the re-settlement program. They were badly beaten and dragged towards us.

They were Aseffa, Tilahun, Seido, and Mekonnen aged between thirty-five and forty-five; they were caught in the confusion, completely unaware what was going on at the camp.

I took a glimpse of our camp for the last time before we proceeded to the deep dense and shadowy forest. At that point, I was not sure if I would be able to come back alive.

Strictly not allowed to turn and see our colleagues at the back or talk to each other, we only heard the words 'go ahead forward' now and then in a very strict and rude manner.

They were in high alert, ready for defense of any attack any time, that made us more nervous, every one of us aware anything could happen any time. There was no guarantee—it was just a matter of when.

Moving in one line, nine of us were guarded by dozens of heavily armed fighters along each side of the line, five in front and many more at the back, driving us like a heard of animals.

Everything was fast, non-stop. It was very hot and humid. Quickly, we become thirsty, sweaty, and tired as we move faster and faster through the obstacles of the forest.

We heard one of them talking through the radio; it was an order from near distance from one of the leaders at the back. We were made to stop for a short break with strict warnings—no talking, whispering, or coughing.

It was our first stop and just over an hour since we left the camp. We became very tired, our mouths became dry with no expression, depressed and completely confused.

At the beginning, it was like a marathon race and not just normal walking. They pushed and kicked us constantly from behind to get us panicked and run faster and faster.

Just before we sat, one of the settlers, Aseffa, came closer to us nervously and whispered that he had his identity card in his pocket and did not know what to do with it.

Aseffa was the chairperson of the farmers' association at Jarso. As one would have expected in his position, he must have been a member of the ruling political party. And it was indicated clearly in his identity card.

It was a serious matter, and there was no time to question. We had to destroy the ID very quickly by any means. As we stood closer in a circle, he dropped it, and we covered it with grasses and soil unnoticed.

For the fighters such indications could confirm they caught the right people. We have to destroy and bury any indication of our connection with the ruling party; else it might cost our lives.

The big question in our mind was, who were these people, what did they want from us, what are their demands were, why all these destruction, why us, why me, and so many such questions.

Approximately thirty minutes later, a sound came through the thick forest—the noise of the fighters. As they got closer, the two white women were easily recognisable followed by their two drivers, all of them dragged by heavily armed fighters and made to sit next to us.

Fiona and Merry, they looked nervous and extremely disturbed. I could not believe my eyes. The two female coordinators of the Irish concern had joined us, and they too had become war prisoners like the rest of us.

Fiona, Marry and two of their employees, Yonnas and Tamiru, four in all, more or less the same age, mid twenties, were sitting next to us and completely confused and unaware of what was going on.

The two women, still in a state of shock, shaking and speechless, were dragged out of their bedrooms at gunpoint. Most of all, they did not understand the language and had no idea what was going on.

Fiona was in a nightgown and Marry was in her pajamas and slippers. They seemed to be totally confused and nervous. They were the only females among us. I felt deeply sorry to see them suffer for something they had nothing to do with.

I thought they would never let them walk five miles in that condition and most probably would be sent back to Sirba 1, Jarso, to their camp. But I was wrong.

They looked at me, and I tried to tell them something, to give them comfort, just by looking through my eyes as if I was talking to them. Be strong, pray hard, you are not alone—that was my message, I was sure they got my message. That was the only way of communications.

Fiona and Marry were entirely dependent on us. Somehow I felt some kind of obligation towards them. I had to do something, just to ease the tension and to comfort them.

Tamiru and Yonnas were the two guys who were kidnapped along with Fiona and Marry. I knew them all very well. They were very friendly, young, and full of energy, but now they all had nearly collapsed.

They also looked frustrated and very confused as every one else. There was a sense of understanding among all of us of the danger and the volatility, just by looking to each other.

We had to forget the past and prepare for the big challenge ahead. We had to have a feeling of togetherness to gain more strength. The situation was very dangerous and unpredictable; anything can happen any time.

Eleven men and two women, a total of thirteen civilian prisoners about five miles away from our camp Sirba 1. The fighters seemed to be relaxed as we moved away further.

One of the leaders came forward pointing his fingers with intimidations and said in a loud voice, 'In this journey if any confrontation broke out between us and the government forces, as a matter of practice it is more likely you would be our first victims.'

The condition had changed dramatically. It become very scary and confusing. From the tone of his speech, we understood as they hade done it previously, nothing would stop them from doing it again.

I think at that moment each and every one of us were asking the same question to no one else but to ourselves. We were innocent civilians. Why did they need to put a death sentence on us? The answer lay in their mind—none of us dared to ask.

Some of us struggled hard not to believe what the leader had just said and created our own version in our minds to ease the tension for a while, that they might use us a shield for their defense, but they may not turn their guns on us.

We all agreed without a doubt that there would be no intensified rescue effort by the government forces neither by those cadres. Even the news will never get to the media. The dictatorial regime of Mengistu is unmatched in recent history of Ethiopia.

Soon we got to our feet and started moving in one line. Everyone of us knew it would be a very long and difficult journey with many risks, and no one could tell us how far and where we should be heading.

Before we started moving, strict warnings were given, followed by intimidations. No talking or whispering. At the start we moved steadily and soon it was getting faster and faster by the minute, thirty or more fighters walking along each side.

It was very hot and humid. All of us were getting thirsty and tired, and they did not allow us to slow down or drink water. They were nervous and weary. They couldn't get off their minds that the army might follow them.

I noticed that one of the fighters was walking at the far front alone as a spy and the rest followed cautiously behind; they did this by turns.

Whenever he picked up or noticed something unusual, he give them a signal. Immediately, they would tell us to sit down or to duck very quickly, and we did as they said.

One of the things that never got off our minds was that we could get killed in some manner by the kidnappers or by the government forces, trapped between the two deaths. There was a possibility, the state security forces might be ahead of us ambushed deep in the forest waiting for us to strike.

In every step we move, there's always be a danger, it was a torture our mind unable to settle and most of all they kept terrorising us constantly to get us panicked to make us move faster.

As is human nature, some of us may not be responsive or fast enough to react to their orders. Whenever and wherever they get a signal, we have to sit or duck very quickly on the spot, although we might be standing on sharp stones, thorns, or muddy water—to them none of that mattered.

If we hesitated to do something or slowed down, they pushed us down to the ground with force and beat us with a stick that was very painful, and whenever they got a clear signal, we started moving again.

Late in the afternoon we came out to the open field. It was time for a short break. They gave us dry biscuits, which they took from the camp of the Irish concern before they burnt it down.

The big questions constantly hammering us were these: where were we going and how far. In addition, if there would be any engagement with the government forces, would that mean the end of us?

About twenty minutes later, they told us to getup and to stand in one line again. One of them said, 'Move quickly, fast,' and frequently these were the only words we heard.

The forest was so dense and tangled with many obstacles that sometimes it was very hard to penetrate and pass through, but we had to do it. We walked non-stop throughout the night deeper and deeper in the forest without a break.

*　　*　　*

Day Two

Early in the morning before daybreak, we emerged out of the dense, misty wet forest to the mouth of an open green field, which stretched for miles and miles.

The big sky and the chain of mountains in the distance offered a spectacular view. It was so amazing. We witnessed the beauty of nature that had never been discovered and was kept hidden.

It was time for a break. After we had the dry biscuits they noticed that some of us had become very exhausted and were not able to move. And soon they left us to sleep for about two hours.

Up again in mid-morning, I felt massive pain all over my body. Very soon we started moving through the stretched plain field. By the time we reached to the end of the field, it was nearly sunset.

I remember walking for hours and falling in muddy waters, in the swampy fields covered with tall grasses. Most of us submerged below our knees. It was one of the worst unforgettable experiences.

The irony was we weren't allowed even to wash ourselves. We slept with our muddy and wet clothes. The nights were very cold, and some of us shivered all night long.

*   *   *

Day Three

It was a clear sky and a bright morning. In no time we entered the dense forest. We did not like to walk in the forest because of many obstacles—fallen trees, foxholes, insects, etc.

We walked through the day with a short break now and then, or when they got signals we stopped as usual. It was humid, and I was sweaty. I took off my shirt. Suddenly, one of the fighters screamed, 'Put on your shirt now!' I did as he said, but I did not understand why he forced me to have my shirt on; of course, it may not have been out of concern for me as a person.

At nightfall, we climbed the steep mountain and descended at the opposite side. When we reached the bottom, every one of us was desperately searching for water to drink out of our bare hands.

We searched for water at the riverbed. It was completely dark. I could not even see my colleagues next to me. Unfortunately, all we found was dry sand and not a drop of water.

I thought there could be a river beneath the huge mountain as one could imagine, but there was nothing. Instead we found just dry rocks and a skeleton of a river. It is hard to describe how thirsty I was at that moment.

On that agonising long journey, we had been through difficult challenges. Especially, shortage of food and water were our main problems. Through that journey, I realised the best way to get rid of hunger and thirst—go to sleep.

Even after a short sleep, I wasn't able to recall the feeling I had moment ago; however, the thirst slowly started to build again as we moved in the hot sun. We got very little amount of water and food once a day.

Throughout our long journey, we crossed several springs and rivers, and no matter how thirsty we became, they did not allow us to drink water. That was one of their unique characters, I hardly understood.

I tried to understand what they might be thinking. Could it be a source of energy possibly for us to escape? Alternatively, it could be their way of punishment to keep us weak. I find it very hard to understand.

Early in the morning, we had a break at one of the mountain tops. They noticed that we had become very weak and were unable to move, so they left us to sleep for a couple of hours.

*   *   *

Day Four

Just before sunrise, I felt someone's kick at the back of my head. It was very painful. Not just me, he kicked all of us. But I was not sure if Fiona and Merry also got kicked. We then quickly pulled ourselves up rubbing our heads. No complaints and no questions, as they told us previously. The guy who kicked us was one of the leaders of the rebel fighters.

I felt pain all over my body. And it was so not just with me—I noticed the expression in every one's face. We started communicating by whispering to each other. We had run out of patience. We did not care about their rules.

We started talking slowly and motivating each other. It was our first time talking face-to-face, but it did not last long. One of the female fighters gave us a warning—'stop talking'.

We noticed that among the rebel fighters, nine of them were females. They were physically very young and energetic, probably between the ages of sixteen and twenty-five.

I was so amazed to see how strong and courageous women fighters could be. It was my first time I was witnessing such a strong character and determination among female fighters.

Sometimes I took time to observe some of the activities around the fighters. The female fighters carried heavy weapons, big pipe mortars, launchers. I did not even know some of the weapons, but it looked very heavy and like twisted steel, uncomfortable to carry.

I was wondering how they could possibly carry such heavy steel for such long distances or what could be the motivation behind all these sacrifices. They may be politically charged with heavy propaganda, but what have we done wrong. After all we're not politicians.

During break intervals and after a long journey, we quickly collapsed, but those female fighters stood in a close range staring towards us with the expression that conveyed the fact that they were far more strong and better than us.

As we covered more and more distance, we became weaker and weaker day by day. And none of us had such exposure in the forest, walking this far and under these conditions.

We did take part in the forest for camping, for the fun of it or adventure, to discover the beauty, but through this journey, we understood the forest was one of the most dangerous places to be.

The fighters were born and had grown up in the forest. They had no knowledge about the civilised world. It seemed liked they were very much associated with the forest, mountains, and rivers, in general with nature. They have little or no knowledge of the existence of the new world.

Even in complete darkness they knew the exact locations of the mountains, the rivers, the thick forests, the plain field, the swampy fields, almost everything They were born in it, they were fed by it, they lived in it . . . forest was their life.

So far, we had been travelling constantly under gunpoint and intimidations. Hile and Marry were the ones who were totally exhausted and dehydrated; often they fell to the ground as they walked.

The rest of us were also unable to walk faster. Frequently, we get pushed and kicked from behind disrespectfully. That was one of the worst physical and mental humiliations.

During the day and at the peak of the heat, we became more thirsty and had less energy to move faster, but at night after the sun got down and when the weather got moderate, we covered more distance.

At the end of day four, at about midnight, we got to a small spring. That was a place to rest. Some of them went to the bushes to collect dry wood. It was the first time they made fire on that journey.

They avoided anything that might expose them or give others indication of their presence. Fire could be one of the signals. As we stretched further, they gained more confidence. They considered themselves to be out of reach. They realised they could not be followed and were confident on their plan of executions.

*   *   *

Day-Five

We never got to sleep peacefully and normally. When we became extremely exhausted, no matter how hard and rocky the surface was, we lowered our body to the ground just to lie down in any way.

When we gotup that morning, the first thing that came to our mind was to drink water as much as we could from the small spring nearby before we started moving again.

Marry started walking on her bare feet. Her slippers had torn apart, and she could not walk fast. They were not happy with her. She was in trouble. Her feet were bleeding. She was sweaty and miserable.

They screamed at her and pushed her. They treated her badly. She had a white T-shirt on at the beginning of our journey. Five days later it had turned dark brown.

The white blonde Marry had been transformed completely, physically as well as emotionally. She was in tears all the time. Very weak she was unable to walk or talk properly.

Unlike Marry, Fiona had shown her strength and was capable of associating herself with despicable and harsh conditions. I think she understood that only the stronger had a chance to survive.

Their two employees, Tamiru and Yonnas, and the three junior mechanics, Faisal, Gecho, and Tolossa, and myself, had become extremely weak and drained physically.

Among us, the four settlers, Aseffa, Seido, Tilahun, and Mekonnen, were in a better shape than the rest of us. I would assume their strength came from their previous experiences in their life. They grew up in farms.

The settlers came to Jarso, hoping for a better life without considering the danger it contained. Unfortunately, they became trapped like the rest of us with no way out.

It was more than seven hours since we had started walking in the hot sun without a break. We felt hungry and thirsty. They noticed that we had become exhausted and dehydrated.

Early in the afternoon, it was time to have a break on the plain field next to a pool of muddy water, which was a natural waterhole where wild animals came to drink.

The footprints of large and small wild animals were clearly visible. We were so desperate for water that even the bad smell of the dirty water did not detract us from drinking.

Merry was trying to filter the dirty water by sucking it through her T-shirt, but one of the male fighters who noticed her doing that came quickly shouting and stopped her from drinking at all.

Most of us were not surprised to learn how these fighters behaved, considering the circumstances and conditions they had been brought up in, but that could not be an excuse. It was a biological effect that we all needed water.

They show little or no respect for human dignity. Sometimes they treated us much less than animals, like war criminals, enemies of their movement, but the truth is that most of us had nothing to do with the existence of this movement.

We started to identify each of the rebel fighters by their names and behaviour. As a human character not all of them were the same. Often some of them were less cruel than others.

The female fighters seemed to be strict and rigid and more of authoritarian than the male companions. In general, they behave more or less the same way, and they still believe we are the enemy.

After we drunk the dirty water and ate the dry biscuit, we started moving again. We became tired of the dry biscuits, but we did not have a choice. We had to eat anything we got in order to survive.

Late in the evening, we were made to rest beneath the terrain of mountains. As we sat together, we started talking to each other, ignoring the rules and regulations; we had got tired of everything.

*　　*　　*

Day Six

Before daybreak, we had our meal, a dry biscuit as usual. As we got up and stood in one line, something unusual and unexpected happened. It was about midday on day six.

One of the settlers among us came towards me out of his line. We all had our positions and strictly there were no change of positions unless they shuffled our positions for their own observation. Suspected escapees always trail behind in the queue followed by snipers.

I was wondering why he came out of the front line. That was a bad mistake on his part. He slowly and calmly came and stood in front of my face, carrying his pair of boots in his left hand, staring at me without speech.

I could sense his desperation to say something very important. He needed to be heard. He was trying to say something he already had decided, but he could not spell it out. He was Mekonnen, the settler.

Clearly, his expression suggested his determination to do something serious and unexpected. It was a dangerous move. I begged him to go back, and slowly he went back to his position without losing sight of me.

I kept on thinking for a while what he was trying to tell me, but I could not figure out. I imagined something dangerous and risky; I struggled to avoid the attention of the fighters.

Soon we started moving steadily through the thick fog and obstacles in the forest. It was about midday. Suddenly, we heard several automatic gunshots followed by, 'Kill him! Kill him!'

Suddenly, all the fighters started shooting several rounds of bullets towards the forest. All of us panicked. It was like a war between two forces. I thought this could be it, the end of us, but it was Mekonnen who escaped.

Most of us noticed him, putting down his head running very fast through the thick bush, zig-zag, from side to side, never afraid to die very courageously, but it was an extremely dangerous move.

We made to stop for a while as they kept on shooting through the bushes in all the directions; they thought he might be hiding. Some of them went searching through the bush.

Mekonnen was not to be found anywhere. They became certain that he ran away with the bullets in his body. One of them said, 'He would be soon dead, somewhere in the bush.'

It became clear to me what he was trying to tell me earlier that day. I was thinking if he had told me I would have stopped him from the decision he had made.

I believed he had made a bad judgment, which could easily cost his life. He might be dead or wounded and left in the bush alone. We do not know if he managed to escape. At the time, it was very distressing to think what would have happened to him afterwards.

Mekonnen had made his own decisions. Most probably he had enough of the harassment and chose to be dead than be treated as an animal; of course, we were all losing hope. We just did not want to die.

Mekonnen, even if he managed to escape the rain of bullets by the miracle of god, had very little chance to make it through the forest alone and empty-handed.

Besides the many risks in the forest, he has no compass to indicate the direction or protection against any incident. It is unthinkable even to go back to Sirba 1, Jarso, where we came from, and it appeared to be very unlikely for anyone to survive.

From the time of that incident, all of us were subjected to new and strict rules. Frequently, we were made to kneel down under gunpoint. They threatened to kill one or more of us just to cripple the idea of escape.

We showed our submissiveness to avoid anything that might provoke them. We assured them it will never happen again, but they did not trust us or listen to anything we had to say, instead they came heavy down upon us.

Soon, we started moving again. Everything had changed—they threatening us, beating us with a stick, shouting and yelling, and driving us crazy. At the moment I thought with certainty that they might kill among us.

Soon we were made to stop and forced to take off our shoes and walk on bare feet. That was a harsh punishment. We needed our shoes more than anything else, considering the thorns and sharp stones. It was unthinkable to walk on bare feet.

A few moments later, they noticed we could not move at all, and they allow us to put on our shoes. It was painful to walk on bare feet and some of us were really counting each step.

* * *

Day Seven

After the incident of Mekonen's escape, we remained under strict control and supervision. No talking or whispering. Even sneezing by accident would lead to punishment. Everything was back to day one.

It was early in the afternoon. While we were walking between the big trees, they got a signal from one of the fighters who usually walked at the far front. Immediately, we were made to stop.

Our life was always in danger. There was always something in the back of our mind, which we could not afford to ignore, which was out of our control. The state forces might be ambushed in the deep forest ahead of us or something might happen any time unexpectedly.

I did not really have the energy to think about all of this. I tried to avoid or not to think what would happen ahead of us, but it was real and could not disappear.

After we stopped, three of the fighters went stalking in to the bush. Soon they came out with two old men and one very old rifle that seemed to belong to one of those old men.

They pushed them and kicked them very hard disrespectfully, and dragged them towards us. They asked them many questions. Before they answered they got kicked; they would panic and get confused.

As we stood we witnessed the cruelty of some of the fighters, the two old men become exhausted and extremely disturbed begging for their life, as they lay on the ground. clearly they were innocent civilians.

The two old men were searching for honey. Honey bees usually make their nest inside the hollow section of the old trees and that was what the two old men were searching for.

For us it was a significant indication that there could be a small town, village, or some human activity nearby. The two old men may not have come from very long distance looking for honey, as honey is available everywhere in the forest.

The two old men belong to the same tribe and spoke the same indigenous language as the rebels, but their identity could not save them. The fighters have their own methods of understanding who they should trust.

The two old men gave away some information about the area, but we did not know in detail. We assumed it was valuable and very important, but I do not think the old men got credit for that.

Soon everything was over, and they let them go without giving back their rifle, but they were too weak to get up and get away. A short while later, we moved away, leaving the two old men on the ground.

It was after sunset and getting dark. Suddenly they got signals. All of us quickly ducked to the ground. We got these kinds of signals frequently; this time it was different.

We climbed up the hill slowly. Just before we got to the top, they gave us quick order by whispering, 'Sit down wherever you are. Strictly no coughing and talking and no movement'.

From the tone of their speech, we recognised it could probably be something they had been scared of for a long time. We also needed to be aware and mindful on our behalf; any wrong move they make would affect us directly.

As we stood, we saw a bright electric light. It appeared to be coming from a small town not far from the hilltop. Our hearts filled with hope; we were very excited about our first experience of seeing the electric light.

Our excitement was short lived. They told us, 'We should go back. It is the wrong path.' Everything started to be fast like a machine. Helplessly we started moving backward. We kept on going, but we did not know how far we should be going.

It was one of the most difficult parts of the entire journey. We walked very fast falling and moving again, non-stop in complete darkness. We became extremely exhausted. Especially, the two white ladies become sick of everything.

Fiona and Merry came thousands of miles away from their country with no political or geographical boundaries, just for one cause—to save human lives. Instead they now needed someone to save their lives.

They were happy voluntary aid workers, kind and willing to assist everyone any time, day or night. I just kept on asking myself, why would this happen to them? Why do they have to go through all these sufferings?

Fiona, although she looked stronger than Marry, also had lost considerable amount of her body weight. The two women still remained puzzled, confused, and weary all the time.

They would have many thoughts about their families back at home. I would imagine how hard and difficult it could be, considering the conditions and circumstances they found themselves in.

Few of us spoke the indigenous language of the fighters, but Fiona and Marry, including the settlers, could not understand their language, and we depended entirely on some of our colleagues for translation.

During that terrible long journey, we became closer than ever before. I think all the suffering made us unite and gave us more strength spiritually as well as emotionally.

Deep in our soul, there was always expectation and desire for some kind of force or a miracle to happen for our freedom. That was just a hope. But that hope never faded away, since the beginning of the journey.

When we came closer to the small town where the light appears unexpectedly, it gave them big shock and they realize they fallow the wrong path that was why they needed to move away quickly in a new direction.

As we have noticed throughout the journey, they tried to avoid bumping into towns or villages or any indications of human activity, which might expose them. There were informers in every town and villages.

We walked through the night without a break, and early in the morning, our conditions deteriorated and we were unable to walk. They recognized it and left us to sleep.

As we lay down on the ground, the scent of the forest, the earth, the odor of the wild flowers was so strange. Even now many years later, I prefer to sleep on the ground closer to the earth.

When I sleep on the ground, I feel more comfort, peace, and calm, but I do not know why. I think I wanted to keep the past alive, which seemed to be not convenient even to remember.

We became very exhausted and were consumed by worries constantly; we were drained physically as well as emotionally. Desperately, we needed everything to end in some way, tired of everything. I had a feeling of worthlessness.

I did not want to think what lay ahead. There was no easy solution, but my brain never settled, thinking and searching for answers all the time. It was not difficult to understand that every one of us was thinking the same thing at the same time without necessarily talking to each other.

It was the first time we slept for a long four hours, beneath the big mountain on a rocky ground. It was one of the most uncomfortable and painful nights of all times.

Some of us who were suffering of pain moaned all night long. We needed someone to turn us from side to side. Most of us were very weak unable to turn from side to side by ourselves. It was completely dark and silent.

I could feel in my back, someone stretched out his arm gently turning me to one side, to this day, I do not know who that person is. I felt helpless. Tears poured from my eyes for the first time. When we woke up in the morning, a few of us found ourselves wet.

During the night, some of us were unable to get up and do the right thing, as we had become terribly weak, powerless, and helpless. It was one of the most horrific and extraordinary experiences.

*   *   *

Day Eight

In the morning, we walked down the hill. We had a feeling that we were heading towards the borderline at the south-west, most probably to their headquarters across the border in Sudan.

Among us, the three remaining settlers, Seido, Tilahun, and Aseffa, are still in a better shape than the rest of us. Although we have gone such great distances, they do not complain the way we do, and they think they are not far from their home, at Sirba 1, Jarso.

We get food once or twice a day, very little, a handful of something just to survive. Since we ran out of biscuits and other dry rations, we got nothing at all. As a human nature, biological phenomenal gradually started to take effect, our thought shifted, craving for food than fear of death by itself.

We began talking as we moved steadily without turning back. For us it was a significant change, a great relief, and freedom of talking has the potential to ease the tension.

We travelled through the day without a break or food. Incidentally, when we came across a river or spring, we took a gulp of water with or without their permission.

We noticed that the fighters got equal or less amount of food than we did. Each of them carried water bottles containing a solution, most probably a mixture of salt and sugar.

In life, we usually take many things for granted, but here that was not the case. We had to ask permission for everything—to drink water or even to turn and talk to our colleagues at the back.

In most cases we got water from the pool, dirty and undrinkable, but none of us got sick out of waterborne diseases, but I am unable to reason why we didn't get sick even when we drank the thick smelly water.

At the time, we did not care about the diseases. Death was all around us anyway, and even now, so many years later, I have great respect for water. Water is life, a precious commodity.

We move forward in complete darkness, following one another like camels. There was no moonlight. It was completely dark. We, including the fighters, became very hungry. There was no food left and nothing to eat.

Whenever we need to do something, we always tried to avoid their attention. We did it unnoticed or ignored them intentionally, but not in a manner of disrespect. In every move we made, we had to bear in mind the consequences.

There was nothing wrong we did except talking or giving signal to each other. Amazingly, we could read one another and express our feelings without necessarily talking.

Late in the evening, suddenly all the fighters came to a halt at once. On our journey, we learnt how to do some of the things. Whenever they stopped, we also stopped immediately to avoid unnecessary intimidations and orders.

On that occasion, we did not get orders to sit down or duck. As we stood, they kept on talking or communicating through the radio, between the front fighters and those who were at the back.

That was the first time we heard them talking loud with absolute confidence through the radio since our return from the small town where the light appears and moving in this direction.

We heard a gunshot just once. It was a buffalo. It took them just one bullet to kill the giant animal. It must have been a great shot, even though we felt sad for the unfortunate animal. We needed protein more than ever.

Subsequently, they divided into different groups. Some of them went to the kill and started to strip the dead animal while a few went to collect firewood. That was the first time we were left unattended on the entire journey.

A sense of freedom returned. A glimpse of hope. We sat in a circle. We talked and expressed our feelings, exchanged views, shared ideas, and drained our pain. We cared for each other.

Collectively we made our commitment, looking eye-to-eye and confirming to each other, to stand firm. Whatever comes ahead of us, to stand together to live together to die together. That was our source of energy.

They left us alone. It was clear that there was no possibility to escape. There were elements of danger in the forest. We did not have the energy to walk even a short distance. They were fully aware of our state physical conditions in general, that we need them more than they do.

They were busy getting the fire started. There was a sense of excitement. They may be closer to their camp to their leaders. They would be congratulated—well-done, good work!

Our main concern was our physical strength and also how much more should we have to go before we got to their camp. And what would be our fate thereafter. We do not expect anything good. We had to prepare our mind for the worst.

A few moments later, one of the fighters brought a huge bunch of barbecued meat carrying on his back and dropped it in front of us on the ground. He said, 'Enjoy your meal.'

We shared the meat among ourselves, and before we ate, we prayed together the first time in one voice. The meat was not fried well and it was unhygienic, mixed with soil. However, we ate everything that came to our mouth.

We needed protein more than ever to gain back our strength. That was the first time we tasted meat, since we started the journey. It felt good, and we ate as much as we could.

The only time we saw and talked to each other face-to-face was whenever we got a break. As usual, after we ate, we started talking softly. We did not have strong voices, but we always encouraged each other.

In spite of all the difficulties and sufferings, we still had great concern and care for each other. When we chatted and smiled, we gained more energy and hope physically as well as emotionally.

After we ate sufficient amount of the meat, we carried the rest in our pockets for the next day; even though it was a mixture of soil, we couldn't afford to waste any of it.

Soon we walked between the fighters freely to get to the fireplace, looking for a softer ground and a level surface to sleep on. They, however, chose to ignore and pay no attention to our movements.

*   *   *

Day Nine

The morning of day nine, we slept probably five long hours. We got up after sunrise. I felt enormous pain in every part of my body as everyone else, but we needed to force ourselves up quickly before we got kicked.

In the mid morning, as we walked through the forest, a sound came through our ears. Welcoming and greetings. The fighter at the front replied, but we did not know who they were talking to.

We noticed the sound came from someone up on top of a tree, who was sitting on the branches. We stopped for a while; it was a chance to listen to their conversations, but we did not know the language. It was different from the one they spoke among the fighters.

Apart from the fighters, a minority tribe lived in the deep forest, distant and forgotten for centuries. They lived deep in the jungle. It was so amazing to discover people who still lived in the darkness, completely out of civilisation.

Their lifestyle was very similar to that of the people of ancient times. They lived in a small hut. They dressed top naked, walk bare feet they practice their own indigenous language and culture, they survived by hunting and roots of different kind.

Their task was to protect the fighters as a shield. They were the eyes and ears of the organisation. From the top of the trees, they looked out for any danger, intruders, or possible attack against the fighters and the camp in general.

In return, the rebels would provide them with food, medical care, clothing, as well as firearms for their security and for hunting purposes. The central government did not even recognise the existence of the tribe.

There is a traditional verbal agreement, which exists between the rebel fighters and the leaders of the tribe. The agreement includes bringing back any escapees from the camp in addition to secure the unclaimed territory of the rebel fighters.

Geographically they are situated between Ethiopia and Sudan. They live in no man's land. However, I strongly doubt if both countries recognise the minority tribe.

Members of the tribe are scattered throughout the forest, covering a large area. It would be difficult and very unlikely for anyone to escape unnoticed. They controlled every escape route.

After short greetings and exchange of information between the fighters and members of the unknown tribe, we moved away steadily between the big trees.

As we moved, we began talking softly among ourselves. One of the fighters showed a sign of interest to talk to us in a friendly manner for the first time with no threat or intimidations.

He was the one we considered better than the rest. He was not aggressive or violent. He was disciplined and sensible compared to some of them who were very cruel, rude, and unkind.

He briefed us about the camp with great admiration, and the rest of the fighters seemed to be agreeing with his non-stop exaggeration, and we listened to everything he said carefully just to understand how their camp looked like.

These interactions might help us to understand what kind of people we were dealing with. Moreover, it would help us to determine what we might be facing at the end of the tunnel—at the camp of the rebel fighters.

They made to believe that their main task would be winning the other tribe and to be separated from the main land, but we do not want to comment on such political matters, simply because the response would be very harsh.

We handled the conversation very carefully to avoid friction. We had nothing to do with their politics. We had only one thing in mind—to free ourselves in any way.

We listened carefully to everything he had to say. It was not difficult to understand how easily they were attracted by cheap propaganda and put their lives on the line.

Under the circumstances, we may be feeling weak, sick and miserable, but not short sighted to see the driving force behind the war above all, the reason why the state of Sudan supports and fuelling the war from time to time. It was a counter balance, the Ethiopian Gov`t supports the Sudanese liberation movements at the North.

We listened carefully, because we needed to ask many questions that were important to us. Why did they kidnap us and what wrong had we done? These are the main questions in everyone's mind.

There is also one last question I needed to ask: Why did they have to capture the two European ladies? However, I could not spell it out. Some of the fighters were unpredictable. They might respond aggressively and most likely break the fragile relationships.

It was understandable the kidnapping of the two women was more likely aimed to attract Western media attention, probably for seeking recognition by the West or for some other reason. Time would tell.

A few questions later, my voice broke. I was so emotional speaking in his tribal language. I was not good in that language, but I needed to speak out to be heard, to express my feelings which affected us all.

We were not politicians nor belonged to any political party. We were ordinary civil servants and government employees, and no one could justify all the suffering we were subjected.

He stopped for a moment and looked at me through my eyes in an unfriendly manner and said, 'We are the liberation front fighting against the oppression of the Ethiopian government.'

Our intention was to let them know and understand that ideologically we were different, and they should respect our point of view, but that was not the case. They liked to impose everything to make us believe by force.

It was not a free discussion. We had to accept whatever they said. It was just one way, and there was no need to ask further questions or pursue our needs. Even expressing ourselves might lead us to aggressive response. To avoid all of this, we shifted our focus and ignored the discussion.

The strict rules and intimidations started to fade away as we approached their camp, but there was no confirmation from the fighters how far we should be going to get to their camp.

It was the afternoon of day nine. We got tired of everything. We desperately needed to end the journey. We wanted justice. We demanded answers. Most of all someone had to be held accountable for our suffering, but deep in our hearts, no one would come forward to take responsibility. After all, this is Africa!

Even now from where I am sitting and nineteen years later and thousands of miles away, I cannot get over the trauma, the effect of the past. It is still difficult to forget the suffering, the anger, and frustration. I found it very hard to avoid or not to have thoughts of the past.

There was a time when Ethiopia was fought against Eritrean secessionists while simultaneously engaged in war against Somalia. Also at the same time the central government had declared a war against the very popular opposition party EPRP and killed thousands of young men and women under the name of 'the red terror'.

Major ideological differences existed among many groups and factions of different political organisations. A few of them pushed their own narrow political agenda based on tribalism instead of promoting the interest of the public.

Thousands of political opponents had been kidnapped or killed. Thousands had been detained and tortured in every part of the country. Many thousands more fled the country.

Late in the evening of day nine, we desperately needed a break. We could not keep up. Among us Haile, Gecho, and Marry were the ones who were affected the most, dragging their bodies behind.

We were told to have a short break. Quickly we fell down to the ground. We never got to have long hours of rest, always rushed to walk again with pain. Endless walk, non-stop pain . . .

As we laid down talking and checking our battered and bruised body. Fiona and Marry, their skin colors have changed, their voices have weakened, among us are those three settlers were amazingly strong.

I had pains in all my joints. My feet were bleeding. I tried to forget the pain, but it was very hard to ignore. When I gave a thought about the pain, it made me weak and unable to walk.

The forest was so green and beautiful; it also contained very dangerous creatures. During our journey we came across many dangerous wild animals, venomous snakes, and nasty insects.

Our clothes were torn apart, our body partially naked and visible, exposed for all kinds of insects. The Tsetse is a species of flies, relatively small and very fast and hard to avoid, mainly found in tropical forests. Whenever they bit deeply, the pain stayed for a long period.

Some of the flying insects followed us for a short distance, and suddenly they were gone. After a while, we got another group of the same kind. It was a constant battle against creeping and flying insects.

The Night of Day Nine

They told us, 'It would be a short stay and strictly no sleeping is allowed.' We had mixed feeling. We did not know what to expect at the end of the tunnel. However, the journey had to end in some way. We thought we might be closer to the camp, and shortly after midnight, we started moving.

Some of us were not really walking. We were swinging from side to side trying very hard to push ourselves. I felt that I run out of energy completely even to walk for one extra hour, but I knew I had to do more than that. Occasionally, we got kicked and pushed from behind.

When we got to the thick bush, I heard someone falling to the side. It was Haile. He always trailed behind in the queue, at the time he was extremely exhausted, out of condition, could not open his eyes and unable to talk.

We made many efforts to get him back to walk, but he was too weak and unconscious and unable to get up even with the support. Finally, they decided, 'We should leave him and move on.'

We complained and declined to walk away leaving Haile behind in the bush, but they threatened to beat us and drag us to their camp by force. We had no power to refuse, except to pray for him in our thoughts.

We talked to him to follow our track which might get him to the camp, even though his eyes were closed and he was extremely dehydrated. We hoped he might be listening subconsciously.

*   *   *

Day Ten

Just before sunrise, we came out to the green plain field, the reddish sky so beautiful—a breathtaking scene. The landscape, the wild flowers, and the birds, everything so natural, untouched.

Day ten seemed to be the last day of the difficult journey. Mid-morning, we came across the big river, the river none of us new previously or had heard about, the Fashim River.

The Fashim River looked like any ordinary river, but geographically as well as historically it has a significant meaning—it served as a borderline, which separated Ethiopia and the Republic of Sudan.

It was not as deep as it looked, just below the knees, about eighty feet wide and flowed gently between the two countries. Soon they made known to us that we had entered the territory of the Republic of Sudan.

Once we crossed the border, the fighters ignored everything about us, talking to each other with great excitement. It was the first time we noticed such great excitement among the fighters.

A couple of hours later, they all went together leading in the front, leaving us behind to follow. There was nothing we could have done, except follow them closely.

We had no other option. We needed to increase our pace to move faster to catch up with the fighters. They walked faster and faster by the minute, and the gap between us was getting bigger and bigger.

No fighter, no more queue in one line, no fear, no orders, no nothing—we were just by ourselves. We gathered together forming one group, talking and supporting each other, following their trucks to the camp, the final destination.

Late in the afternoon as we got closer to the camp, we heard several gun-shots repeatedly from a distance ahead of us. It seemed to be from our side of the fighters.

Moment later, we heard the sound of a blast from a far distance, which seemed to be from the camp. It was their way of greeting and welcoming the fighters. It was one of their biggest achievements.

The gap between the fighters and us were increasing, and they stretched for about a mile. Ahead of them in a distance, we discovered smoke coming out of small huts made of hay. Unexpectedly, we become energised stimulated by the atmosphere, and we start moving faster.

We put aside thinking of our future and everything for a while we have one thing in mind, to get to their camp we were not going to our homes or to our families, but to no-man's land to the danger zone, the leaders of the rebel fighters waiting for us for more interrogations.

As we got closer, we noticed the movement of people, and shortly the fighters joined their comrades at the camp. It was time for celebration and confirmation.

We dragged our battered body towards the camp very slowly, walking side by side freely on the open field and waiting for some of our colleagues who were sick and remained far behind.

By the time we got to the camp, some of them were playing netball. We could see several light and heavy firearms scattered unattended. Perhaps there was no need to safe guard as no one else, except them.

At last, we reached to their camp and that brings to the end of the long journey for a while, the camp did not have a fence or entrance gate or no distinctive mark. Slowly we joined the new fighters and many of them came with eagerness to see how the war victims looked like.

Immediately, two of the rebels guided us to one of the tiny huts. At the corner of the field, silently we stepped in trailing one another. At that point, we had no idea what would happen next.

Those fighters who brought us there had completed their mission. They handed us over to the new fighters at the camp, and that was the beginning of a new chapter.

THE HEADQUARTER OF THE REBEL CAMP

'The Fashim Camp'

South Sudan

Fashim is the name of the area, particularly the territorial region, between the two countries. None of us knew the exact meaning. It was probably drawn from the landmark, the Fashim River.

We were given away to the fresh fighters, and those old fighters slipped away and disappeared to the inner parts of the camp through the bush to their camp leaders.

They would be congratulated, received a heroic welcome, and probably, they may be given medals for their success. Soon they will be sent out again for another invasion, to different places. Next time they may not be lucky. They may never come back. There may be no glory.

After ten days and more or less 300 kms of difficult and exhausting journey, we at last made it to the Fashim camp, the camp they all were proud of, the headquarter of the rebel fighters.

We sat closer in the tiny hut with no talking, smiling, or expressions, just looking one another silently for a while. We had mixed feelings. We also had physical and emotional pains.

Someone broke the silence. We started talking and re-discovering each other. We had lost significant amount of our body weight. We became so weak we were not even able to stand.

We prayed deeply for our dear friends. Mekonnen the settler who escaped during our journey and Haile, who was left behind the previous night. Finally, we thanked God for the strength he gave us.

It was about half an hour since we had arrived at the Fashim camp—nine men and two white females sitting together in a small empty hut wondering how had we made it through.

We needed to rest and did not want to see any fighter for a while. We wanted to be left alone; we could hear the excitement and enthusiasm among some of the fighters who gathered outside of the small hut.

A short while later, two fighters came in, and one of them said in a loud voice, pointing his finger, 'You two must come with us,' and they took them away in a hurry.

That was a very sad moment for all of us, Fiona and Marry turning their back weaving their hands with out a word, disapeared very quickly fallowing the two fighters, some of us did not even notice.

I was thinking for a while, do they really heart them more. Alternatively, they might use them for media publicity or demand ransom money. None of us knew the answer; we just assumed.

Fiona and Marry were originally from the powerful states of Europe. There would be consequences. I was sure the bosses of the rebel fighters should take good care of them.

Shortly two men came in carrying boiled beans and water with dirty plates and cans. We ate the food and drank the water together. We were hungry. We did not care about the taste or hygiene.

Normally I do not feel hungry early in the morning, but on this journey we became hungry and thirsty all the time. Soon we stretched our legs and fell asleep in our torn clothes. I was so deep in sleep, even the mosquito bites did not shake me up.

We had to learn and adopt some of the things that many of us had never thought before—eating unhygienic food, sleeping naked on the ground, in the rain, cold, hot sun, insect bite so on . . .

Since the beginning of our long journey it was the first time we slept for long hours, it was our first night at Fashim camp, very cold and uncomfortable, and the small hut did not have door or windows.

During the night while we were sleeping, many fighters came in and out several times. I heard once, but my colleagues noticed so many times. Whoever came it did not matter.

The next morning four people came in and stood looking us down. There was not enough space to accommodate all of them. They told us to go outside on the green grass. We did as they said.

One of them stepped up and said, 'From now you are under strict control. You are not allowed to speak in your own language. No political discussion and no contact with any of the fighters.'

The next speaker said, 'You would be given a political lesson and sooner or later you would become part of us, joining our struggle, for our freedom and prosperity.'

We may be forced to accept their rules, but it would be impossible to remain silent. We showed our refusal in one voice. In fact, we were quite the opposite of their ideology.

As we understood from the tone of their speech, they may have had something in mind. They needed our support to keep us here to feed us political propaganda, and be part of their struggle.

For us it was unthinkable, beyond imagination, but it was an indication that we would remain in detention for a long time under their control, at least until we agreed to or challenged their proposal.

The four men were the political cadres of the movement of the rebel fighters, it was depressing to find ourselves under siege, from fascist cadres to other ones, we do not like cadres we had bad experience.

They liked to impose everything on us after all the painful experiences we went through. Here again we remained under strict control. They insisted whenever and whatever they wished.

Before they left, we needed to ask the questions we never got answers for. We all said in one voice, 'We are innocent civilians and not politicians. We need our freedom we want justice now.'

Probably, they may not kill us certainly. They would try other means and ways to get us to be part of their political struggle. Moreover, they needed our technical skills badly in many of their segments.

We needed to calm down and shift our thoughts and pray to our dear colleagues Haile, who remained behind in the bush, and Mekonnen, who escaped during our journey.

Haile was working as a store man at Jarso (AMSC). A very peaceful and respectable person, I was very close to him. We had many conversation about our past while we were at Jarso peacefully.

He withdrew his study from Addis Ababa University due to personal reason he was a third-year student, Shortly he got this job and trained as a store man. That was how he came to Jarso.

I met him the first time at Jarso. He was at 'Sirba 1' two months prior to my arrival. He never mentioned about his family or his backgrounds. He was polite and liked to keep everything to himself. Most of the time he preferred to be alone and did not want to mix with people.

Shortly after we completed the praying session, one of our friends, Tolossa, noticed a shadow of someone coming from outside. For our safety, whenever we saw a shadow or someone coming from outside, we stopped talking immediately.

It was Haile, who emerge behind the shadow. He followed our foot track and his natural instinct, and at last counting his steps, he made it to the camp. He was listening subconsciously to everything we had said to him.

Ten of us stayed together in that small hut. It was about five days since we arrived, and during our stay, no one was interested to talk to us. It seemed like we had got to the dead end.

The living conditions at the detention camp was extremely poor, unhealthy, and disgusting—no proper sanitation, unhygienic food and water. As a result our state of health got bad.

The camp was built in such a way for protection against any attacks from the air or ground, swallowed by the thick bush and not visible even from a near distance.

We do not know exactly how it looked from the other side of Sudan, but I would imagine it should be very large camp and divided in to many different sections stretched deep in the forest.

Each section has its own leader and security forces. It was the main head quarter of the rebel movement presumably the place where the planning, strategies and all kinds of logistical matters discussed.

It was one week since we arrived at Fashim camp. One evening three fully armed men came in a hurry. They told us, 'Get up quickly and follow them', and we did as they say.

Soon we crossed through the inner part of the camp. We came out to the open space, the place where with a lot of secrecy meetings took place between the leaders.

We stopped in front of a small hut that extended from the bigger segment. Soon two women with long dresses emerge from the inner part of the hut. They were Fiona and Marry.

They cried in tears weaving their hands in mixed reactions, very exited most probably they would be sent back to their country, at the same time they were sad because we remain behind in detention not knowing our fate.

It was the most unforgettable moment in my life. We were warded off in a short distance and could not be able to talk to them closely and freely, however we have displayed the same emotions.

We shared many painful and life-long memories with Fiona and Merry. I still remember clearly those moments so many years later from where I am sitting now.

For the time being, we forget our own problems, and we become excited and happy for them to be free and join their families. They insisted and demanded that they need to see us for the last goodbye.

Fiona and Marry came thousands of miles away from their country for one cause in mind—to give life for the dying, the destitute, and the needy. True heroes, great women. They would be remembered for the good work they have done in the settlement areas.

It was very unfortunate they were caught between the dirty wars and such fatal consequences as we all were aware they had nothing to do with our internal politics and conflicts.

At last we said to them, 'God bless. You are wonderful. Wherever you go you will always be remembered. We are proud of your bravery, fearlessness, and courageousness.'

We were then taken away very quickly back to our hut. it was a moment of dark And dull, full of sadness, silently we prayed in our heart for the two brave women's Fiona, Marry and Mekonnen who escaped during our journey and for all of us.

One week later, we were transferred to another section within the camp, and we were placed on the open space in the hot sun, cold, and rain with no shelter This was done deliberately as a punishment for our refusal to join and support their struggle.

We remained on the open space for a week. Our biggest challenge was the rain and the mosquito bites, especially when it rained during the night and in a complete darkness with no shelter or protection. It is difficult to explain how bad it was.

Gradually our state of health deteriorated the condition become unbearable. I remember one specific event. We stood up most of the night as the rainwater flooded beneath our feet. It was impossible to sit or do anything.

After the rain had gone, the war started against the mosquitoes. They came in huge numbers and were unstoppable. They penetrate through our torn clothes piercing our skin; it was very irritating and unavoidable.

After a week's stay in that condition, most of us suffered of high fever and experienced constant vomiting as the day progress, we become weaker, exhausted to the extent unable to walk even a short distances, distressed and hopeless, difficult to describe.

As a human nature, the one thing I realised was how strong we can be when confronted face-to-face with the big challenges. The sprit of fighting back took over for survival, thinking positive,we tend to forget the past specially the bad once very quickly.

The situation was very volatile. In order to survive, we needed to adopt and adjust ourselves to see the next day and be ready for the next challenge. There was no time to mourn.

We learnt to forget quickly the previous one, in order for us to be ready and be mindful of the next one. It went on and on . . . endless challenges. I think this is the time to remember and drain everything, which has been sealed off for many years in my mind.

One week later, we were transferred to one of many different sections of the camp. The camp has many sections and sub-sections close to each other covered with thick bush.

The new section was different from the previous one. We stayed inside the shelter. It had a roof, but all sides were open. We remained inside the shelter for about a week without going out.

This section was much better than the previous ones. We did not get sunburnt during the day and drenched in rain at night, and we had a chance to observe and study the activities of the fighters openly.

As we noticed, there were very few of them who showed concern about our condition and were not happy the way we were treated by the some of the rebel fighters, but they could not speak out; however, we understood and appreciated their feelings.

It may be strange to communicate through expressions; we all have the same view over some of the fighters, but as a human kind all of them were not the same. We were able to identify from their behaviours and attitudes how some of them were extremely unkind and evil.

As time progress, we associated ourselves with the surroundings and began to understand the social life and activities of the rebel fighters at the camp while they were not on duty or fighting. Regularly they engaged in different activities. There was no free time.

Daily political lesson is compulsory for every member of the party. After the session the propaganda followed, which was highly intensified specially within the fighters.

Preparation for the next invasions and few of them go to the smaller towns and villages deep in Ethiopian territory spying and gathering information, which were valuable for the next operations. We had learnt that everyone was active day in and day out doing anything.

We got tobacco leaves whenever we asked the fighters. That gesture improved our social relations with some of the fighters. Some of us used to smoke, and we had to learn how to roll and smoke tobaccos. Our benefit was more than to share the tobacco, subsquently it made us closer to the fighters and that was what we looking for.

Before and after we transferred to the new section we had been visited by various kinds of people. They usually came and went. I think they just spied on us, but we had no secrets and nothing to hide.

Our interaction between the fighters grew from time to time, creating trust and enhancing our moral. It was a window of opportunity, and constantly we kept on pursuing on this line of communication. However, there were risks, which could not be ignored. One of the rules said 'do not talk with the fighters.'

It was the second week of May. On a Sunday morning, two gentlemen came in with their bodyguards to our hut, and they introduced themselves as political cadres of the organisation.

They came to preach political propaganda by force, but we had our own burning issues, which was, why were we here? And at the time we were not prepared to listen to any political non-sense.

We were not interested to listen about their tribes or their distorted version of Ethiopian history at gunpoint; we had better knowledge about the history of our own country.

Before they started their agenda, we started by firing direct and confrontational questions, but they chose to ignore everything we asked and never bothered about any of our demands.

The next day in the morning two people came in, apart from the previous ones, and demanded we should follow them very quickly with no explanation. We followed as they proceeded, and soon we arrived at another section.

We have identified some of the fighters, immoral and responded negatively and aggressively to any of our demands. Such harsh behaviour and rudeness discouraged us from asking even the simplest things. However, it requires a great deal of patience and high standard of discipline in order to achieve our long-term vision.

We needed to be closer to the fighters. They were our lifeline, not all of them, but some of them. We did not want to remain in the dark. We need information to understand our future.

The cadres, comrades, section leaders, and administrative workers are those who did not want to talk to us. They responded suspiciously for everything we asked, and they usually avoided eye contact and kept us in a distance; deep down they knew we were innocent civilians.

When we got to the new section, one of them showed us a small hut, pointing his finger towards the corner of the section. It was the same as the previous one but different in size and shape, with no walls, and it was our fourth shelter.

We didn't know why, and no one dared to tell us why they need to transfer us from time to time, from section to section, from shelter to shelter. We had to follow wherever and whatever they said.

Whenever we went to a new section, we became tired of new bosses, new rules, and new restrictions from time to time. Soon they gave us a kind of food, boiled beans in a small plate as usual, just to survive.

After we ate our food, the leader of the section came to our hut followed by two of his armed bodyguards. He was one of the most feared and was known for his cruelty. One of the reasons they sent us here was as a punishment for our refusal of their political lessons.

Through our experience the leaders of the sections seemed to be very strict and serious. Whenever they took a walk through the camp, they had always been greeted with great respect and dignity.

The section leader gave us instructions, 'You would be required to do a job. You cannot stay idle any longer, and those of you who defy our orders would be dealt with severe punishment.' This was followed by intimidations.

The next morning, four fighters came in with several axes and empty 20-liter buckets to carry water and cut the wood. They handed the material over to us as usual. We followed them as the two fighters led from the front.

When we got to the open field, we were made to stop and subsequently split into two groups—five of us went to cut the woods and the rest had been assigned to carry water from the stream.

For some time, this practice remained our main task, twice a day in the morning and in the afternoon. Sometimes we took turns and some of us went to the river as the other group went to cut the woods.

Each person had to carry two buckets of water at a time. We hooked the water buckets to a piece of long stick to each end for balancing, and we carried them across our shoulders.

The fighters allocated which one of the trees should be cut and decided who should carry the smaller or the bigger tree depending on our strength. Each of us had to cut at least one tree and carry it to our section, which was about two miles away.

One particular day as usual, we came from the bush carrying woods and water. As we approached our section, we noticed unfamiliar people in military uniforms standing in front of our shelter.

I turned and asked the fighter at the back, we have developed fair relationships with this particular fighter who do not hesitate to give us some information, which are not sensitive. I asked him, 'Who are those men?' He replied, 'They are the military forces of the Sudanese government.'

Some of the fighters were very kind to answer some minor questions; soon we joined the military people. We witnessed those men belonged to the Sudanese army.

The five military men approached every one of us with careful observation without speech as we stood next to the water buckets. We looked at them. They were very tall, muscular, and with shining dark skin.

One of the questions in our mind was 'why did they come to us' and 'what did they want from us.' We had our own assumptions; most probably, they came for inspection purposes. They needed to prove whether the rebel organisation is doing the job to the expectation—kidnapping, torturing, and terrorising innocent civilians.

As we stood they came closer to us and silently observed each and every one of us moving from side to side. They kept staring towards us without speech, we had many questions to ask to speak out, but we are not allowed to do so, however we shouted and screamed disrespectfully out of frustration, but none of them gave us attention.

Short while later the the Sudanese army shoved away along with the rebel fighters as we stood. It was a bitter feeling to have been considered as war criminals by the old enemies of Ethiopia.

Beside the Nile River, Sudan is among the Arabian countries who regarded Ethiopia as the enemy of the Arab nation. Due to the diplomatic ties with Israel, Ethiopia has a bad image in most Arabian countries.

The rebel fighters were supported and trained by the Sudanese government and provided with territorial and logistical support, where they built their camp and prepared and intensified a guerilla war against Ethiopia.

As time advanced, we become closer to some of the fighters who regularly took us to work. In the process some of them divulged secrets of the camp innocently, one at a time; however, we are not their enemy, and we did not hunt for their secrets. What mattered to us was to find a clue to our freedom without getting hurt.

Some of them expressed their personal experience without considering how dangerous it could be for them to talk, and for us to listen; however, that little information helped us to build our hope.

We needed the inside story. We had to engage with fighters closely to get to know them better. This might open the gate to develop good friendship and respect and these interaction might help us to understand how likely they could keep us in detention.

We did not have any defensive strategy. We were captives. We did not have any kind of right. We did not even have the right to speak in our own language. We had no control over anything. We had to find other mechanisms even to communicate among ourselves.

Usually we did not plan for anything. In actual fact we did not have anything to plan, but when things were getting tougher and when every door was closed, our mind activates to find solutions.

We suffered immensely at the hands of the rebel fighters. We witnessed how they behaved, cruel, not having a feeling of guilt, odd characters; however, we could not afford to distance ourselves from them. We had to obey with great respect.

We need to understand their thinking Their discussions and decisions concerning us, although we did not have any influence on them we could not settle until we understand what likely our fate could be. Some of my colleagues had good experience in handling difficult people in difficult conditions.

I believe as long as we kept on breathing there is always hope. It may not be bright certainty, but we hung on to any hope; otherwise we may be thinking of something different, which may not be reversible.

As we understood most of the fighters were forced to join or snatched and trained as child soldiers without their will or the consent of their families. They were told they should fight for their independence. That may or may not be true, but I do not want to get in to that kind of politics.

Every morning whenever we go to or from the job, carrying axles and water buckets, commonly we follow the same path, but one morning the guard suggested a different idea, a quick way to the camp, a short passage. He was the one we trusted the most.

He led us through the inner part of the camp. Shortly we came out to a field, half the size of a soccer field, and we had seen a few heavy trucks scattered on one corner of the field.

Slowly we passed to the opposite corner of the field as we carried buckets of water and wood. When we observed closely, we noticed some kind of activity. The big dark trucks did not have registration numbers or any indication where they came from. Our guard told us, 'They're donated by the Sudanese government.'

Those trucks were carrying many young children of both sexes, between the ages of six and twelve. Some of the kids were crying very loudly as the armed fighters surrounded them.

We witnessed the fighters constantly intimidated the young kids. We slow down our movement to observe from a short distance. For the fighters it was a normal duty, nothing unusual; for us it was disturbing. Some time later we shoved away unnoticed.

The guard insisted we should move quickly. We understood his concern. He said, 'To witness such incidents would carry consequences. It would be bad for you and bad for my reputation as well.'

Among the few fighters who were close to us, he was the one who had shown a great concern about our condition and who passed some information to us about some of the things.

At a later stage, we understood those kids were kidnapped from the Ethiopian territories forcefully by the rebel fighters. They would be raised and trained as rebel fighters, and they will be sent back to fight the dirty war, doing the same thing as their masters, abduct other kids. It was an endless cycle.

At the end of June, we got to the point we could not wait any longer. We needed to stand up and do something. We needed to shake up. We needed to push them to decide. We did not care for the outcome. We had our own meeting, and in the end, we decided to go on a hunger strike.

We called the head of the section; we pronounce collectively our decision to go on a hunger strike and our refusal to work, until we got answers for our demands.

He tried very hard to scare us away from the idea of a hunger strike, but we had enough of the suffering, we stood very firm and unshaken by his threats and make him realise, his threats would never change our mind.

The next morning the authorities came to talk to us with many kinds of warnings and threats instead of answers, but we stood together firmly with confidence. None of their threats would detract us from our decision.

Our demands were the same as usual; we called up on our release urgently. We needed justice and freedom now! They would take us back to Ethiopia or any country freely.

They went out for a short meeting and came back with the new strategy. They said, 'The highest body of the organisation would make the decisions about your future and you will be notified by next week.' That was their final word, and we ask no more questions. Shortly they went out and we were left alone and depressed.

We decided to terminate the hunger strike for a while and wait for the answers. Some of our colleagues were affected by malaria. Wavering and weak they were unable to walk even short distances.

Two days later the leader of the section came to our shelter and called two of our colleagues Tolossa and Tilahun, and he took them away without any explanation. We started to be concerned.

Our main concern was that most of them did not want to communicate with us. Whenever we asked questions, we did not get answers at all, and that made us frustrated.

Since from the day Fiona and Marry were taken away there was always concern in the back of our minds. There was no news and no one willing to tell us about their fate, but we talked about them regularly.

It was about two weeks since the disappearance of Tolossa and Tilahun. Our concerns were growing. Since there was no news, we kept on asking, but our effort was not successful.

Gradually we developed good relationships and trust among many of the rebel fighters, but they also did not know the fate of our colleagues and their whereabouts. That was very disturbing.

Gecho was one of our colleagues who was never afraid to speak out. He usually expressed himself angrily. Whenever they came to us, he became increasingly furious from time to time.

They regarded him as a crazy person. He started to show a sign of weird and abnormal characters talking alone, short of memories and it was no surprise one could behave differently considering the circumstances.

Not only Gecho, but some of our colleagues also were not the same as they used to be. There was a feeling of hopelessness, emptiness, vacuum, with some of them unable to talk sensibly.

One morning Gecho came to where I was sitting. He wanted to tell me something unusual. He looked at me in to my eyes, and after taking a deep breath, he said, 'I lost every little hope and do not want to live any longer.'

As the going got tougher, he gave up and told me in a short and depressed sound, 'He has decided as the last option to end his life and he felt that was his time.'

I was shocked. I never expected him to have such a thought, but I was very glad he had told me. He could have done it without telling anyone. In those circumstances we may all have the same thought at different times. I think we kept to ourselves sealed.

Such thoughts could have the power to damage our morale extensively, and if one leads, some of us might develop the tendency to follow the same action, and that would be disaster.

I need to find a way to destruct or divert him from such bad thoughts and I had to be careful, honest, and straightforward, but there was no guarantee. It was difficult to read the mind of a human being.

I told him my own true feeling instead of supporting or rejecting his idea. For a long time I thought about suicide, but I kept it to myself, just like my security.

We do not have to make emotional decisions. There may be hope, and I believe sometimes something good might pos up unexpectedly. After he listened everything of my hidden secrets, he become aware that he was alone and most probably everyone one of us thinking the same thing at different times out of desperation, but none of us talked about it.

The reason why I was more close and concerned about Gecho was because he had told me his personal life history long before the tragedy happened, while we were at Jarso peacefully.

He was born in a poor family. He had two brothers and a little sister. His father died while he was ten years old. He was the eldest one and had to take care of the younger brothers and the sister.

Soon after his father passed away, his mother committed suicide due to heavy depression for many years. As a result, at the young age, Gecho became the breadwinner and was responsible for the family.

At the time he was a student at primary school and after school times he used to sell goods on the street to provide food for the family. That was how he grew up raising his brothers and sister.

After he had completed his studies at a technical college, he got employment and was posted at 'Sirba 1', Jarso, as a junior mechanic and that was how I came to know Gecho.

Towards the end of July, all of us became sick of malaria. As a result we became weak and could not go out of our shelter as we normally did and some of the fighters noticed our condition and notified the leaders about our state of health.

The section leader came to our shelter and tried to give us his side of advice by saying, 'If you join us, you will be provided with good medical care, food, and other benefits.'

We made it very clear that we're not interested in the kind of politics they're running. Above all, we do not believe in tribal war and we we're not willing to participate in their struggle.

On numerous occasions, they talked to us in a persuasive manner, but we strongly refused to join them. We had witnessed so many bad things since we came to that camp—torture, killings, child abductions, terror, no freedom, and no consideration or respect for human rights.

Eight of us remained intact in a small shelter, and there was no news of Fiona, Marry, and the three guys Tolossa, Tilahun, and Mekonnen, the one who escaped during the journey. We hoped they would be fine. We prayed for everyone of them wherever they were. We did not have any information.

The leaders and many of the fighters avoided any kind of questions regarding the disappearance of our colleagues, but desperately we needed information because it would have given us an indication to our future.

As we become closer to the fighters we also become aware that, there are spy's among the fighters who observe secretly and closely, who give out any kind of information to the leaders,' invisible people'.

Lately, we were allowed to go to the river once a week to clean ourselves, with two or three guards. We do not get soap, but we were happy to break away for a while from controlled environment to the natural river.

It was one of the rare moments. We talked to the fighters freely. It worked both ways. It was also convenient and a comfortable condition to release their hidden emotions. They had many stories to tell to someone; they needed to be heard.

On many occasions they do talk to us freely, and these interactions helped us grow our relationship further. In the process we have understood and discovered many secrets of the organisation.

As time went by, we become very weak, but the two remaining local farmers seemed to be strong and better than the rest., Asseffa and Seido had lost considerable amount of their body weight.

Myself, Gecho, Faisal, Haile, Tamiru, and Yonnas, and the two farmers, all of us got sick of malarial diseases—vomiting, high fever, and headache; our conditions deteriorated as the day progress.

Finally, we were given medication in the form of injections and tablets, which had expired many years ago. Since then gradually all of us recovered and fortunately the expired medicine worked.

We entered the third month since we were kidnapped from Jarso, and most of the restrictions were gradually removed. We could walk and talk freely only in designated areas.

There was a sign of peoples who were kidnapped and detained at the camp previously, but we do not know their fate and no one willing to tell us the truth, if they were dead or still alive.

One morning we discovered something very shocking and disturbing—several human skeletons and bullets cartridges scattered everywhere in the bush, neglected.

Shiny white and clean human skeleton washed by the rain, visible from a distance. It was probably there for many years. I would assume it would be there for many years to come.

Since that scene, I never got to sleep properly for many nights. Eventually my head started shaking frequently. My colleagues told me that it could be a nervous problem.

At the beginning my head shakes for couple of minutes and stops and after a while starts again. whenever I become tense, it stars unexpectedly I have tried very hard to control the shaking, it was impossible.

Gecho advised me to calm down and not to be stressed out, but it was very hard to ignore and relax, particularly in that condition. I had to make time and disregard some of the bad images.

We noticed that the Ethiopian army invaded the area two years prior to our capture and destroyed the entire camp killing many rebel fighters. And this camp was rebuilt again exactly on the same location.

There was always one big question floating in our mind. It was about the remains of those victims—why was it abandoned and not buried? For us it remained a mystery and we did not want to ask.

During the envision by Ethiopian Government forces, the rebel fighters retreated back to the inner part of the Sudan as a strategy, hiding all food items, weapons and valuable materials underground. Occasionally, we got such information from one of the fighters who remained close to us.

When the war was over, they came back in numbers and built the camp from the scratch all over again, assisted by the Sudanese army who provide all the materials and skilled work force.

The food we were given was the food which was hidden underground. It was unhygienic—the beans mixed with soil and insects boiled together in one big dirty pot. That was our meal once a day.

The food should not be for human consumption, and we did not have the appetite, but we had to eat. We wanted to survive. We had hopes. We did not want to die. There was always a little hope deep in our souls.

We imagined, one day we would be free to tell our story. That was the hope we had, it feels like very unlikely that to happen, however we kept on counting the dates, waiting the next day a miracle to happen, waiting and waiting . . .

It was the first week of August. Sitting outside in the sun, we saw someone coming to us. It was Tilahun, smiling from a distance. When he got closer, we all got up and gave him a hug.

It was good to see him alive. Some of us were suspicious. We needed to know the conditions, and how and why they decided to return him back. Due to the circumstances one had to be cautious.

Shortly we started firing questions—where and why they took him, why was he not convinced by their propaganda, what did they discuss about our future, and about many other things.

Tilahun the settler, uneducated and unskilled, did not speak their language and may not communicate very well, but for us he was a very lovable, kind, and innocent person.

He told us, 'There was a great deal of hope. They might let us go freely.' But he was not sure when and how. He got the information from one of the fighters, among those who kidnapped us from Jarso.

Suddenly we become energized, our mind activated, the little hope we had grew rapidly, our soul stimulated, we live in hope, Tilahun remained loyal and honest and has never change his character.

He told us the bad news about our colleague Tolossa who was taken with him, 'Tolossa becomes the new member of the rebel fighters and he could not be with us any longer, he was one of our colleague, but now he has changed, he become one of the fighters.

Furthermore, while Tolossa was here, he was spying on us. We had secrets among us at one point. There was a discussion between us of a possible escape, but we dropped the idea because it was impossible.

At that time, Gecho and I were accused of inciting and provoking a hunger strike and subjected to severe punishment differently from the rest of our colleagues. We had never thought Tolossa would be a traitor.

Gecho and myself were made to kneel down on sand as a form of punishment, carrying twenty-liter water buckets on each side of our shoulders, for about an hour with short intervals.

For several days Gecho and myself have tried to get answers, why the two of us punished apart from the rest of our colleagues, what have we done wrong differently, the rest of our colleagues did not have the nswers.

We found out Tolossa was the one who gave away every little secret and information we had to the leaders. At that time, we became angry. We felt deeply betrayed and very disappointed by the action of Tolossa.

Tolossa was one of our junior mechanics at Sirba 1. He belonged to the tribes of the rebel fighters who claim 'part of the region belongs to them and fighting for their independent' that was according to their statement.

They shared a common language and culture. It was not difficult to attract a person like Tolossa, but he could have refused and taken a stand like the rest of us. I think he wanted to save his own life disregarding the rest of us.

After Tilahun joined us, we became nine men again. It was the second week of August, and one afternoon, unexpectedly we had a big surprise,—we had visitors, four armed men.

They came to see us purposely with a smile and greeted us with respect and dignity above all, with new attitude. They were among those fighters who kidnapped us from Jarso. It was the first time we met since they handed us over to the camp, nearly three months ago.

They approached us differently with no intimidations or harassment, instead with different expression. They became shocked and deeply saddened by our appearance and felt guilty, partially because they knew what they did to us on the long journey from Jarso to Fashim.

For a while, they kept silent, observing closely our physical state. They noticed we had reduced dramatically and had become weak, fragile, and worn out. They knew we should not be targeted, but they had no political power to stop it.

Nothing would have changed that, they have to carry out the orders of the leaders. In this business, there is only one-way of communication, from top to bottom, there is no vice versa. The four visitors promised to pass on any information's regarding our future.

We had a feeling of enthusiasm and excitement but did not know why. We needed to be sympathetic. As we talked we have discovered the other side of the rebel fighters, honest and caring, but they had to carry out orders, and when they did, they behave differently, very cruel, beyond expression.

There was a growing rumor about our release. We sniffed in every corner of the camp to get adequate information and more information was flowing from our sources. Previously, a number of innocent civilians had been killed by the kidnappers.

There was always doubt in our minds. Would it be possible to get back our freedom? Would they let us go freely? In terms of the speculations as to what they did in the past, it was very frightening. They never let anyone go freely.

We had nothing to pack and were psychologically filled with excitement and moral, ready to move any time anywhere, but did not have the strength to walk even short distances.

We did not know exactly where and when we should be going. We become certain. We would be going very soon, long and difficult journey. At the time we did not concern about the distance, as long as we get our freedom.

Early in the morning on Saturday, 27 August, we heard footsteps of two young fighters as they approached our hut. The order came, 'Step outside, and in one line.' When a call like this came through, everything had changed, a reminder of the past, a reminder of movement.

Immediately, we began to feel the energy, strong intensity, and enthusiasm. Excitement was rising our hopes rises to the highest level, because We never ever anticipated to happen unexpectedly. we got-up to our feet and stood on one line'. The question of where was not important at that point.

From Fashim to Nowhere

Day One

We strolled out as they stood at either side of the small hut and lined up very quickly as we used to do, eager to get going as quickly as possible, to get out of Fashim.

'Here is your document,' said one of the fighters, my ID card, passport and my bank cards were among a few documents handed over to me, which were taken from my house at 'Sirba 1' Jarso, before they burnt it down.

Some of my colleagues got nothing of their personal items and none of us were concerned. There was nothing more important than life, the excitement building up by the minute, and we could not wait to move.

The second fighter said, 'It was decided, you are free to go, and for the next two days we will guide you the direction, and you will proceed alone and freely through the forest.'

The mood in the camp was different, excitement and as we proceed some of them are watching us from near distance, among them are those fighters who're close to us, we understood their concern. They may have a doubt if we could make it through. We promised to give everything of ourselves.

We started moving. They led us from the front. We followed them behind. They were young and strong, cruising very fast through the toll grasses, and we followed them closely at the start.

As we advanced through the forest, we started to fall away and the gap between us increased as the two fighters stretched ahead. Most of us were sick and vomiting constantly, unable to catch up.

The two young fighters were kind and fully aware of our state of health, but from time to time, they insisted we should walk faster and follow them closely. Gradually they become agitated and very strict. We could not manage to keep up and walk fast.

One of our concern was, we had no food to eat The two fighters got a kind of maize powder wrapped in a piece of dirty cloth, swinging across their shoulders, which could last for two days.

They also had a concern. They still had to return back to the camp. The maize powder would not last long. Probably that was the reason they pushed us over the limit to get us move faster.

They needed to get rid of us, throw us somewhere and get back quickly. Their clock was ticking; we knew they had been given limited days. We also knew the leaders were very strict when they execute their plan, and there was no trust in this business.

Once we left by ourselves, we would be able to put all our minds together collectively. We would make use of the forest for our survival. Wild fruits, roots, and hunting were on the menu.

We had survived the most hard and gruesome punishment in the hands of the fighters. It was incomparable, and that was our measurement for any problems we might be facing ahead and beyond.

As we progressed in slow motion, by mid-day we had a short rest far from the camp. There was a feeling of happiness, excitement, and freedom. Gradually, the mood was changing positively, creating momentum, driving us forward.

As we stretched forward, we gained more confidence and morale. We could talk and walk freely; we thanked our creator who gave us strength, kept us alive, and guided us through the forest.

Before sunset, we came to the level ground. It was time for a break. Soon we spotted a small hut standing alone with a very clean yard. As we moved closer, we also noticed there was an old man standing in the yard.

We went into the yard following the two rebel fighters. And we made ourselves comfortable as they talked with the old man, and from that point, we did not require their permission.

Shortly, the three men agreed that we would be spending the night in the yard under their protection. The old man belonged to the tribe who controlled the movement of people from or to the camp.

Three months ago, when we came to the camp, we crossed the Fashim River. I thought now we were moving in a different path. We must have been moving parallel to the river in a distance and out of sight.

We sat in the yard wondering how everything changed in a matter of a day. Between our conversations, something caught our eyes, several chickens running around. Our thought shifted quickly. We became hungry just like animals. We did not get food for the last two days even before we started the journey.

We requested the old man politely to give us one of the chickens. He replied, 'Get any one you want and make yourself food.' We caught one of the chicken, but we did not know what to do with it.

The three farmers among us, Seido, Tilahun, and Aseffa, knew how to make food. Without wasting time, we started the fire. We learnt from the fighters how to make fire by friction, by rubbing two sticks, one against the other. We made a big fire.

The old man gave us maize powder, a clay pot, and water. We made our own supper. And that was the first time we tasted real food, since the kidnapping took place more than three months ago.

We become free unexpectedly without pre-condition. Some of us were afraid to sleep or could not get sleep, preferred to sit and talk the entire night. Soon, a few of us fell asleep around the fire.

The weather got hot during the day and mild at night. Even when it rained, the temperature remained moderate to our advantage. It was the middle of winter season.

*   *   *

Day Two

We got up early in the morning. We felt much better, our minds fresh. We wash our hands and face. The old man gave us tobacco leaves, wishing us good luck. Shortly, we proceeded and disappeared through the thick and misty forest, following the two young fighters.

The old man was a guard, to keep an eye and monitor for any intruders. The two fighters were our insurance, our passport. If we were alone, the old man would have treated us quite differently.

We would have definitely been tied up and taken back to the camp, and without any doubt, we would have been killed and our remains would be left scattered in the bush as we have witnessed.

As we got underway through the bush, I asked one of the fighters why would the old man live alone in the forest, and how would he be able to survive alone.

One of them replied, 'The old man was not alone. There are many of them in the bush. They observe your movement closely, but you would not be able to see them.'

I had no more questions. Slowly and silently, we vanished following the two rebel fighters. The only way to get out of the radar was to get going faster and faster.

The winter grass was so tall, the two strong fighters opening and cruising the thick bush in the front as we followed them closely behind. That was our last hope, do or die! Sooner or later, we would be left alone to find our way by ourselves.

We were heading to a very small village across the border to the Ethiopian territory, but we do not know how far we should be going and that was the first time they indicated the direction we were going.

We could not keep up with the two young fighters. They ran out of patience and changed their attitude, threatening to take us back to the camp. Some of us became very exhausted and trailed far behind the rest of the group.

The two fighters, very much associated with the forest, knew exactly the location of the mountains, the rivers, and the direction, during the day and at night.

The two fighters seemed to be not talking to each other frequently, but when they did, it was soft and short, alert and ready all the time cruising silently very fast through the forest.

Insects were everywhere of different sizes, shapes, and colour. They flew, crept on the ground, and we got them everywhere, even in our food and water. We ate them, we drank them.

The area was located in the equatorial region and the forest was hot, humid, and conducive for reproduction of insects. I never had a thought insects would have such a tremendous effect.

Late in the afternoon, before sunset we needed to rest. That brought the end of the second day's journey. At the same time, we were out of the surveillance area and one-step closer to the real world to civilization.

Suddenly, the two fighters stopped when we got to a piece of land, which appeared to be cultivated at one stage many years ago. A clear indication, people may have lived there a long time ago.

Further away, the two fighters were discussing, seemingly a matter of importance. Shortly one of them said, 'This is our last point. We should be going back to the camp, and you have to find your way out.'

That was good news totally to be free, but we're not certain if we could make it through, not only the distance, but it could also be dangerous to move in the forest empty handed without clear directions.

One of them came forward by pointing his fingers and tried to show us the direction from the very distance. The giant shadowy chain mountains were visible many miles away.

'You should go over those mountains, and when you get down to the other side you would get a River, after you crossed the River and climb the hill you would be able to locate the Ethiopian village'.

They said, 'If we could walk fast enough it could only be about two days to get to the village.' They also mentioned, 'We should be aware of the danger, ambushed Ethiopian army.'

Our hearts filled with hope. We made a commitment that we would make it, but two days in our current condition would mean four days, far too long for us to walk without food and protection.

As we stood, we discussed and shortly came up with the idea, 'If they could guide us just for one extra day, it would be a great advantage to us.' But they refused to go further one inch from that point.

Instead, they gave us a huge bundle of pamphlets, written in their language, political propaganda. We should distribute them when we get to the Ethiopian village. It was the last order.

During that time there was no democracy in Ethiopia, anyone who would be found oposing the state or spreading political activities against the government, would mean a death sentence.

The flyers which were given to us could serve as a travel document, if we came across to any of the rebel member or supporters, but it has a risk to carry such materials which was banned by the state and every one of us aware of that.

We decided to spend the night on that plain field the first time freely with no rebel fighters and no restriction, since the day we were kidnapped from Jarso, the morning of Thursday, 28 April 1988.

The two fighters quickly disappeared through the forest back to their camp without saying a word, not even goodbye, as the mail carrier who delivers a package from one point to another.

We all belong to different religions back ground and whenever we pray,we pray collectively, we observe one creator, one God, among us one of the settler, Aseffa leads the pray session and we follow, 'thank you God'.

*   *   *

Day Three

As usual, we got up early in the morning, and at that time of the morning all of us felt hungry. We had to follow the survival methods. We needed anything, which could give us the strength more than ever.

The three local farmers, Aseffa, Tilahun, and Seido, were the ones who look strong and more confident among us. We had our commitment: should any one of us got sick, injured, or faced any danger, we would stand as one and defend together.

W proceeded through the forest led by the three farmers, looking out for wild fruits. When we got one, first we analysed if it was safe and non-poisonous before we ate.

At midday, we came across to the small spring, we do not need permission to rest or drink water, no one telling us what to do, but we're fully aware the danger, we need to get out of the forest as fast as possible, we have to move.

We decided to destroy those flyers and threw them into the spring. We could not possibly carry a message, which could put us in more trouble. None of us were interested to read what it said as there was no need to do that. We knew it carried a political propaganda.

So far we had tasted different kinds, shapes, colours, and size of fruits. The forest is rich in fruits and they are available everywhere, but we could not survive just by eating fruits—we needed protein.

The first day gone quite well, everything looks promising, when we go down the hill and closer to river it was like sinking in the forest, covered with thick forest and impossible to see the giant mountains ahead of us.

By the time we got to the river it was flooded, rising and widening by the hour, and impossible to cross to other side. There must have been heavy rains somewhere far away in the mountains. We decided to spend the night by the riverbank.

Before it got darker, we collected dry woods. We had learned how to make fire. Fire is our savior, our protection. We made a big fire. We believed it would drive away any dangerous animals.

It gave us hope, a feeling of confidence. Sometimes we carried a portion of fire inside the hollow section of bamboo trees, for the next break. Fire was the only weapon we had in hand.

The night was bright full moon, the forest contains so may creatures, echoing different kinds of sound from different directions, everything was so natural and beautiful.

Some of us were not sleeping and were partially awake all night long. Although it looked beautiful and peaceful, we had to be aware of the danger. We did not know exactly where we were. The green beautiful forest is more likely to be full of surprises.

Since we started this leg of journey, my head shakes less than it used to be, but I still have the feeling of uneasiness, but I am getting better, we have a vision and hope. My head shakes not only when I freaked—out, but occasionally it starts when I get excited as well.

Day Four

Early in the morning before daybreak, everybody showed eagerness to get going to move fast. And we discovered the river had gone and very little water flowing. I think the river had sunk in to the sand.

It was the fourth day since we began the journey and second day by our own. We felt very free, eating our fruits and climbing the steep mountain upwards very slowly, counting each rock and tree.

Climbing, resting, and moving again, it took us the whole day just to get closer to the top of the mountain. It was nearly sunset. We became very tired, hungry, and exhausted.

It was time to rest, time to make a big fire and collect fruits. Haile and Faisal became weak and unable to walk; slowly, they emerge dragging their battered bodies to the level ground where we sat.

As we sat around the fire, our supper was fruits of different sizes, shapes, and tastes—sweet, sour, bitter, while some of them tasted like leaves. We chewed everything that came to our mouth.

Despite all the problems we had, it was the combination of excitement and the thought of heading towards the dream village that gave us the appetite and energy to move forward.

The dream village none of us knew or heard about may not be far, but we did not have the direction. Sometimes we doubted if the dream village even existed.
The two fighters may not be wrong or they may have been lying. We asked ourselves, do they really care about us? Of course, they are humans, and at least they did not let us get lost in the forest.

Soon all of us fell asleep as usual, partially awake for any possible danger. We did not expect any human presence, but we were afraid of the wild animals—buffalos, lions, snakes . . .

Our heart filled with hope and our minds were travelling hundreds of miles away. We started to imagine our future, how would our families react when they saw us, and what would they feel when they discovered what we went through. What would be their reaction? Nevertheless, the little hope we had was growing by the day.

Every move we made ultimately brought us closer to reality; eventually, our dreams would be real. As some of us slept, some of us were talking throughout the night, talking about our families, friends, about everything.

*   *   *

Day Five

It was our third day since we separated from the two rebel fighters. They should be at their camp by now, but we do not even know our destination. We just have to make every effort to get going. There was no time to spare. We had to make a move.

Two of our guys became very weak and were unable to walk and that was a big concern. We encouraged and pushed them to move forward. On the other hand, the three settlers at the front were getting tired of us. We walked slowly and not as much as they would have liked us to move, some us in the middle trying to pull both groups together.

Sometimes they got frustrated, but they were not leaving us behind. They were just encouraging us. Occasionally we took a turn to open the thick bush at the front. The bush was so thick and tangled, someone had to open or make a hole at the front following the direction of sunrise, to the east.

The next destination would be very crucial for our survival; we had to get to the dream village, desperately any village, to any human activity. We ran out of everything.

That morning we climbed up the huge mountain, we were not sure if that was the mountain where the two fighters pointed out from the very distance, before they went back to their camp.

By mid-morning, we get to the top and rest on the flat surface. Soon Assefa, one of the farmers, noticed something different from the very distance.

He discovered very small trees on top of a hill and next to the trees. He also noticed a piece of land, dark brown. We all stood up to figure out the miracle, but the trees were too small to be recognised from a distance.

He said, 'Those trees are the eucalyptus trees, and that piece of land is fresh ploughed land.' The two farmers seemed to be agreeing with the new discovery. I hold my breath. I did not want to be excited so quickly.

To find eucalyptus trees among the forest trees makes it very significant. By nature they do not belong to the forest trees. They could only planted by humans, and we concluded that there had to be someone out there.

There must be a village around the tree, and if there was a village, there must be people. Suddenly, we become energised, and we had to get to the trees, to that piece of land, to the dream village.

We started moving down the other side of the mountain and disappeared into the thick dark forest. When we reached the bottom, we felt like tiny creatures, crawling beneath the huge mountain. It was very difficult even to understand which direction we came from.

One of our big problems was H. Mariam and Faisel who could not move any more. Their bodies had given up. That was a major setback, which affected every one of us. We cannot continue our journey leaving anyone behind.

Faisel was a soccer player at a young age. Many years ago, he had a leg injury. It had healed completely, but now so many years later the pain had come back and he could not move his left leg. That was our major concern.

We had to move slowly, to give him a break now and then. He begged us to leave him alone and save our lives, but we refused and walked slowly side by side encouraging him. It was getting dark, and we needed to rest again.

As we rested, some of us tried to get the fire started. A few of us went in different directions in search of something to eat, perhaps anything. What I found was very surprising, the coffee trees.

The only explanation I could give was that perhaps the coffee seeds might have been dropped by the birds. Any way I collected large amount of the red coffee beans, and that was our meal. We hoped the last meal of the journey.

During the night, no one goes to sleep, thinking and talking about those small tress and the brown piece of land, could not get off our mind. We had strong feelings of getting closer to the village, to any village, to human presence.

Day Six

When we got up in the morning, we found ourselves beneath the hill. And we were not quite sure exactly if that was the hill we were looking for, where we located the eucalyptus tree. Early in the morning, slowly we started climbing the hill inch by inch.

The hill was not big or steep to climb, but the problem was with us. We didn't have energy even to get up from our sit. By the mid afternoon, we pulled ourselves to the top of the hill, and we discovered something, which took our breath away, the giant eucalyptus trees.

As we emerged one by one, those old massive trees were in front of us, very big and majestic, standing in straight line, on top of the hill, peacefully signaling for those who may have lost in the jungle forest.

Those huge trees were very small from a distance, it was difficult to identify and singled out from the rest of the forest trees, but Aseffa and the two farmers have previous experience to identify, even from the very distance. Next to the trees was a piece of fresh ploughed land, the brown land.

At that point, our body gave up and unable to walk an inch and all of us fell to the ground never to get up again, until some one finds us, but not the rebels fighters, some one has to take care of us.

All of us started crying and were speechless, overwhelmed by emotions from where we lay down certainly. There has to be a village and desperately we need some one has to see us, our last hope.

We trusted the eucalyptus and followed the signal, as if it pronounce, 'Come to me, and you would be saved.' Without any doubt we were saved by the eucalyptus tree.

The New Beginning

Ethiopian Territory

Shortly we pulled our neck from where we laid down, and we discovered a smoke coming out from the small hut in a near distance. At the same time, we saw someone coming towards us.

When he got closer, he noticed something was wrong and started to run away backwards. We tried to call him back with weak voices. He listened and cautiously he came back again. He thought we were the rebel fighters.

After he calmed himself down, he approached us with close observation before he talked to us further. He asked the first question moving towards where we laid down, 'Are you not the rebel fighters?'

We said, 'No, we were kidnapped by the rebel fighters.' He then apologised and said, 'Because you look like them.' We understood why he feared the rebel fighters even if they became weak and were unable to walk.

He felt sorry and ran to get more assistance from the nearby village, and at that point, we become emotional and all of us broke into tears. I really do not have words to describe our feeling at the time.

The man belonged to the indigenous tribe of the fighters and spoke the same language of the rebel fighters. This specific tribe is the largest population in Ethiopia. It was a confirmation we entered the Ethiopian territory.

We lay down totally powerless and very weak. Shortly the villagers arrived and carried us to the village, and we were made to lie down under the big tree in the center of tiny village called Torri.

More and more people gathered from every corner of the village climbing, one on top of the other, just to get a glimpse of us and speak to us in their language.

They shook their heads and cried. One of them said it was a miracle. Some of them came with food, coffee, tea, cigarettes, clothing, just anything to show us their support, but we did not have the appetite.

One of the elderly men among the villagers began praying out loud in a strong voice. Suddenly the crowd went quiet and down on their knees. We all prayed, thank you god!

The villagers were very caring, kind, and warm. They noticed our condition—shaky, fragile, exhausted, and powerless. They were amazed. How anyone possibly could survive and managed to get to Torri village?

First, I did not want to accept the reality. There was a feeling of doubt within myself. Could it be true or just a dream? A powerful thought against the reality. For a while, I didn't want to think about the past.

I asked one of the villagers standing to my side, 'What is the date today?' He replied, 'Wednesday, 27 July 1988.' Exactly three months and fourteen days since the drama began.

If we draw an imaginary line, Jarso to Fashim and Torri, the entire journey would make up a triangular figure, with one side missing, which is Torri to Jarso. The longest would be about two hundred and fifty kilometres. And the shortest would be Fashim to Torri.

A short while later, the Ethiopian army heard about our arrival and they came in numbers to the Torri village and carried us away to their barracks, which is about five miles away from the village.

The barrack is located on the corner of small town called Bisho. We were then taken to the town clinic for medical examination before we went back to the barrack where we spent the night.

Bisho is a small town located at the south-west end part of Ethiopia, about seven hundred kilometres away from the capital Addis. There was no direct road link between Bisho and Jarso.

Bisho is a small town. It has two primary schools, couple of restaurants, and shops. The road from and to Bisho was seasonal. Transportation is possible during the summer season. The road to Bisho is impossible during the rainy season.

There was no telephone line, and communication is possible only by means of two-way radio transmitter from the army base or police station, which is for the purpose of security reason, and not for public services.

We spent the night at the army barracks, but we didn't like the environment to be closer to firearms or anything-sound military, we need to stay far from such things, we need peace of mind and calmness.

Early in the morning after breakfast, we held a meeting. The head of the army needed to talk to us, but we did not know why. Shortly, he came with the ruling party leaders.

The leader of the army had good knowledge of the exact location of the rebel fighters at Fashim and different sections of the camp, the detention points in general. He had all the information.

Most of all how the fighters infiltrated through the forest unnoticed causing extensive damage to the property; moreover, the psychological damage they caused politically and militarily.

By the time of the invasion and after the kidnapping took place, the military has surrounded the entire region. As he describes, 'I could not understand how the fighters slipped out through the tight security control.'

From previous experience he has confirmed what the fighters intended to do during our journey. 'If the army had engaged fighting with the rebels, your life definitely would have been in danger.'

I thought we would have been left dead and rotten in the thick bush, along with the rebels if the army had found us. We were very fortunate the army never found us. The army leader has well established intelligent services that is able to infiltrate rebel territory, gathering information, but nothing has been done to our advantage.

Finally, he told us how very close we came to death when we crossed the no-go area unnoticed, the Gov`t army has a base hidden in the forest, beneath the hill of the Eucalyptus trees and it is well known by the communities at large, and no one dare to be closer to the 'danger zone'.

The army leader tries to persuade us to stay in the army barracks for a while, but we rejected his idea collectively and strongly in one voice. We made it clear our refusal to stay in the army barracks for one more day.

They guided us to one of the small hotels in the town center. We did not want to stay separated in the army barracks. We suffered together. We need to be together in order to recover from emotional and physical pain.

The communities at Bisho came to see us at the small hotel where we stayed temporarily. Some of our visitors were the schoolteachers, nurses, students, young and old. They gave us everything we asked for—clothing, food, and carrying us when we needed to go to the bathrooms . . .

*   *   *

The next morning we heard of someone coming from outside and asked, 'Where are they?' with a sound of excitement, of someone particularly recognisable to all of us.

It was so amazing. We all got shocked to hear that sound. None of us really expected to hear in a million years, the sound of the young man who escaped during our journey, Mekonnen the settler.

He stepped in to our room with a smile, extremely happy to join us again, Mekonnen the settler, alive and well, who was considered to be dead and forgotten in the bush.

We were thrilled and over-excited to see him alive. He looked at every one of us closely, one by one, and gave us a huge hug. He noticed that three members were missing—Fiona, Marry, and Tolossa.

We told him everything from the time of his escape—what the fighters did to us and how it happened. And it was a moment of prayer for all of us including for those who left behind, Fiona, Merry, and Tolossa.

After our prayer, we asked him how he managed to escape the rain of bullets and make it to Bisho. It was very unlikely for anyone to come out alive considering how the fighters control every move we made.

Now it became clear. Bisho was the town which we spotted from the top of the hill the night before Mekonnen's escape. Bisho was the town of the bright electric light.

Every one of us had bad memories specifically of that night, which cannot be forgotten. They turned us away, they said, 'It is the wrong path. We should go back to the junction.' It was one of the most difficult nights of the entire journey.

Mekonnen escaped unhurt miraculously. He thought about escape from the beginning, waiting for the right moment. That morning he made his decision out of hopelessness and desperation.

He put his head down running very fast, zigzag, turning sharply, from side to side, through the thick bush without turning back. About two miles later, he become exhausted and collapsed under a big tree.

After he escaped, there had been a great deal of confusion, and the rebels abandoned the search very quickly. They thought we might get a chance to disperse and escape in different directions. On the other hand, the condition created a good opportunity for Mekonnen to stretch further.

Late in the afternoon, after we had gone long ago, he began to memorise the direction of the small town bright light, the one we spotted the previous night, and he followed his instinct.

When he gets to the top of the mountain, it was after the sunsets and moment later, the darkness took over and nothing was visible except the one thing, the sparkling light of Bisho Town from the very distance.

He spent the night on top of the mountain, could not sleep, scared and alone but at the same time, very excited. He knew he was just miles away from reaching his dream. The next morning before sunrise, he went down to the bush thinking of the shortest route to Bisho.

There were no tracks of humans. He had to remember and memorise the directions carefully including where he came from. Once he got down to the tall grasses, it would be difficult to find his way out or back to where he started.

At about twelve noon, when he got to the outskirts of Bisho, he met people and informed them how he managed to get there, and they took him to the police. Eventually, the police noticed a stranger who came from far very distressed, exhausted, and not able to speak the local language.

When we found Mekonnen, he was absolutely healthy, leading a normal life at Bisho. Originally, he came from the northern part of Ethiopia through the settlement program.

All the settlement areas including Assossa are protected with roadblocks and checkpoints, to stop the flow of the settlers back to their origin where they came from. This applies for Mekonnen as well.

Mekonnen joined us and we become ten again. For the next three days we stayed in a single room together. However, we had difficulties to sleep during the night—nightmares, horrible dreams, feeling of chocking, suffocation . . .

Some of my colleagues screamed all the night afraid to sleep. Usually we sat and talked most of the night. It seemed to be a psychological problem. I think some of us did not get the reality deep from inside.

There was no counseling or a professional who dealt with such cases. We did not get help in terms of the psychological problems. Some of my colleagues thought it would diminish as time progressed.

Most of us affected emotionally inflamed with anger and traumatised, gradually it began to surface affecting in our day to day life, as the matter of fact, so many years later, I 'm still angry of what we went through and in my opinion, 'time never heals'.

Three days later, it was time to move out from Bisho. Before we moved out, I need to report our safe return to the head office based in Assossa, to the general manager of the AMSC, to a man called, Mr Mulat.

Assossa was about more than two hundred miles away north-west of Bisho, and communication is possible only by means of two-way radio transmitter situated at Bisho police station.

I went to the police station and met a police officer who already had been informed about our return. I handed over to him the message, which I intended to send, but the radio transmitter would not function properly.

I left the message for him to report on our behalf. He promised he would try his best to get the message to the manager at Assossa, AMSC head office as soon as possible.

*   *   *

In the first week of August, all of us were packed in an old Land Rover pick up car and headed to the provincial city called Nekempt, hundred miles away, leaving Mekonnen behind at Bisho.

Mekonnen told us he would prefer to stay at Bisho Town and did not want to go back to Jarso. He had already established a small business and had a partner. He was single and did not have a family at Jarso. That was the last time we met him, Mekonnen the settler.

We became nine again. Later in the afternoon, about half way, the Land Rover developed a minor ignition problem, and we were forced to spend the night at the roadside. That was not a big deal, but it seemed the forest does not let us go without problems.

The next morning the Land Rover was repaired. And in the afternoon, we drove to the city of Nekempt where the governmental and regional party leaders' offices were located.

We were taken to the office of the provincial ruling party leader. He was at his office sitting with some of the intelligent men. After short greetings we were pushed to go outside by three armed police officers.

At the time, our physical appearance was quit different from the normal persons'—uncombed long hair, unshaved beard, weak, walking funnily . . . easily recognisable as crazy people.

Nekempt is highly populated relatively. A big city saturated with big and small shops and big hotels, known for its moderate temperature. And it is one of the tourist destinations in the western part of Ethiopia.

Shortly, we were taken to another office, the office of the intelligent services. And as we sat at the reception, I was called at first, and he let me sit in front of him. He then started talking, waving his hands, seemingly to express his anger.

I was more confused and puzzled by what he said. 'We know all about you. We have enough information. You came here to spy for the terrorists.' He goes on and on . . . all false accusation.

I said to myself, 'Is it a kind of a joke or our problems are not yet over? I was very frustrated and angry and losing hope. We were absolutely innocent, yet we were considered as suspects'.

At last he said, 'If you do not confess the whole truth, you will be detained indefinitely and subject to torture.' I looked at him with disbelief. I had a feeling of hatefulness and bitterness in my mouth.

Before I moved away from the chair, I said to him, 'We all are innocent and have nothing to do with the politics. We came out of death's mouth. I have nothing to confess.' And we were interrogated and humiliated one by one.

Gecho and Haile didn't say a word. They kicked them, they pushed them, but they remained silent, numb, and the rest of my colleagues were confused and didn't know what to say. Finally, we were told to step outside.

We were disappointed, deeply hurt, and depressed our hopes were dashed, our dream had faded away. Despite all the difficulties we went through, we're defined as enemies by both sides. Who are we then? What would be next?

I had to swallow my personal emotions. I hade to think very hard to bring about calmness among us. We needed to find a way out from the misery. We needed to talk and whenever we started talking, we felt better.

Whenever I became tense, my head starts shaking unexpectedly, seldom It makes me sweaty and tired and I have to force myself to calm down in order to stop the shaking. I have learned how to control and make myself calm down.

Whenever we face a bigger challenge, we stand together as one great family to deal with the problem and minimise the stress; we care for eachother, there is a strong bond among us, which kept us togather.

We were left in the waiting room for long hours. They were having meetings and discussions, which ultimately affected our future in one way or another. We did not want to go to prison.

Those intelligent men regarded us as the agents of the guerilla fighters and that perception worried me very badly, and in such a case, no one would want to come forward to defend us.

Even the trust among our old friends who were not kidnapped might tends to be doubtful, uncertain about our current political status, they distanced themselves, fear of the implications and the consequences. After all, it is a political matter. People might change their view and align themselves with certain political group.

Even though we were completely innocent and out of politics, it was the risk and the matter of the state secret services most people scared to interfere specially, when the case appears to be related with the rebel fighters, many people do not want to interfere.

Late in the afternoon, we became hungry and bored. We started to complain, run out of patience, to show them our unhappiness. We felt it was time to stand up and raise our voices, to speak aloud.

We shouted collectively. We screamed non-stop out of desperation. We could get attention. Sooner or later something must happen. We cannot wait. We were innocent.

Many people from the Town start gathering hanging over the fence to find out what was going on, we look like some kind of animals in captivity, many of them seems to be wondering, where we came from.

Shortly, two people emerge from the meeting. They told us to follow them to their vehicle. They took us to the city center to one of the hotel. One of the men informed us, 'We have found out that you are free and not guilty of anything.'

I was thinking why would they mess with our emotions. They knew and they had all the information about us, the exact location of the rebel fighters, about Jarso, about Fashim, about everything.

We came out from the detention at Fashim rebel camp and what else now, some of my colleagues tempted to ask in a challenging way, but none of us opened our mouth. We always had fear of negative response, inviting more trouble.

Just before they left, one of the men mentioned, 'If you require any assistance regarding your safety and necessities at the hotel, we're willing to provide, but will not apologise for the interrogation as it was part of our job.'

We shouted collectively, in one voice, 'We do not need your assistance. Do not come again. We do not want to see you.' I do not think they had a feeling of guilt of what they have done. Soon they went out without turning back.

It was a good hotel, but some of us had difficulties sleeping on soft and comfortable bed. It may take time for some of us to adopt modern living. Personally, I prefer to sleep on hard surface on the floor. It sounds crazy, but it gives me more pleasure.

The next day as usual we got up early in the morning, and shortly after breakfast, there was someone, a visitor at the reception waiting for us by the name of Zewde Teferra.

Zewde is the head of administration at Assossa, AMSC. He was likeable and known by every one of us and a close friend of mine. We spent good times while I was in Assossa.

I had many good memories with Zewde. He has a tendency of associating himself with everyone very quickly. He has been always disciplined, gentle, and caring. He was likeable almost by everyone.

Zewde could not recognise any us for a while. He shook his head silently in disbelief observing our physical state, as he stood between the chairs. He felt deeply sorry for what we went through.

He said, 'I was sent by the manager on a rescue mission'. We understood the news of our release already spread by the police officer who is a radio operator stationed at Bisho.

All of us looked terrible. I lost over one third of my body weight. I became skinny and unrecognisable. It was one of the most unpleasant feelings to be unrecognisable by close friend and that was the first time we met since I came from Germany.

The next morning was the second week of August 1988 and we began the long journey back to Assossa, to the head office of the AMSC.

We drove through the day. Late in the evening we get to a small town called Nedjo, and arrangements had been made prior to our arrival. We were then taken care of by the head administrator, Zewde. We spent the night at small hotel at Nedjo.

Nedjo is a junction on the main line, 80 miles to the west, before Assossa and about 30 miles to the south to Jarso village, connecting Addis, Jarso, and Assossa.

The next morning we need to make a turn to get to Jarso. It is about two hours' drive from the main road. In the afternoon, we reached Jarso, the settlement area, the starting point, where the drama began.

The communities at Jarso settlement area already heard the news prior to our arrival and gathered to welcome us, including the families and friends of our three colleagues, Aseffa, Seido, and Tilahun.

After the kidnapping took place, the AMSC already abandoned the entire regional operation. This included Assossa and Jarso as well. During our tour, we did not see any of our colleagues, those who escaped through the fences at the time of the invasion.

The Jarso settlers knew exactly what we stood for. Our main objective was to cultivate the land and assist the settlers to bring about change to improve their life in the long term, not running politics, as we were accused of both by the state and the rebels.

Silently, we tour through our camp to observe the magnitude of the disaster. It might give us an indication, what went wrong, why, and how it happened, which way they came in, and which way they took us out of the camp. These findings might help us to understand the event which took place the morning of Thursday, 28 April 1988.

I could say there was no camp. There was nothing left of the camp—ashes, plain field covered with grasses. I went and stood at the exact location where my house used to be. There was nothing left of my house, ashes covered by tall grasses.

I remembered the exact position where the fighter stood calling me to get out. It was a moment of deep sadness. I discovered cartridges of exploded ammunitions and remains of burned rifle.

My colleagues also occupied on their own thinking with sadness standing on the remaining of their living houses. We have the time even to investigate how some of our colleagues escaped through the fence unnoticed during the invasion. Shortly we went to the camp next to ours, the camp of the 'Irish concern', Fiona's and Mary's camp.

Literally, the fire consumed everything including the big tents where large quantities of materials were kept especially for emergency needs. Medicines, dry foods, and blankets are few of them. Commonly outbreaks of diseases occurred from time to time caused by poor sanitation in the settlement areas.

We have witnessed the remaining of their living hoses and the skeletons of their vehicles partially covered with tall grasses, as they stood on the same spot, ready for the morning service, which never took place.

Instead, they stood silently as a ghost, as a reminder of the event of Thursday morning, 28 April 1988. I could not stop thinking, sometimes things do happen suddenly and unexpectedly in a blink of an eye, and the effect would be devastating and the scars last forever on the minds of the victims.

The change appear gradually afterwards with slow motion as nothing has happened. The beautiful green grass grew rapidly on the fertile soil on the remains, on the ashes.

We moved out from the devastated area and went to the families of our three colleagues to spend some time. Aseffa, Tilahun, and Seido. The mood in the village was quite different from the empty camps. Their families never thought their husbands would come back alive, as there has never been anyone who returned previously.

Most of the settlers questioned about the disappearance of the two young women, Fiona and Marry, with great concern. They were loved and respected as their own and always remembered for the good work they had done.

We told them everything what we went through, but we had no information since they took them away one morning. We hoped they would be fine and most probably taken away to the country of their origin.

It was time to say goodbye to our dear friends, the three settlers, Aseffa, Seido, and Tilahun. They are our heroes, guiding us and opening the thick bush at the front and encouraging us to move forward during hard times, and most of all, they are the ones who spotted the eucalyptus tree, 'our savior'.

Aseffa was the chairman of the newly formed farmers' association at Jarso and that was a major concern for his wife and two kids as the rebel fighters were looking for people who held positions in the public sector or government.

Tilahun was the youngest among the three settlers. He was innocent and full of energy. He was taken away with Tolossa but returned back, while Tolossa remained in the hands of the rebel fighters while we were in detention at Fashim camp.

A couple of weeks later, Tilahun came back alone, leaving Tolossa behind, who betrayed us. Tilahun was the one who came with the good news and the first time we sensed the indication of hope of our release.

Seido whose real name is Seeid, the tallest among the three settlers. He was quite, gentle and confident on himself, do not necessarily argue with any of us. He was like a big brother, master of the jungle.

The remaining six of us—myself, Faisal, Yonnas, Tamiru, Gecho and Haile—headed for Assossa. We spent the night at the junction, at a small town of Nedjo, where we used to come for shopping once a week during the good times.

The next morning we drove to Assossa, which is located north-west, far end, of Ethiopia, which is about less than a hundred miles from the border of Sudan at north.

Assossa is a big town rather than a city with many hotels and restaurants, different government offices, and is known to be one of the oldest towns in western Ethiopia.

At the time, Assossa was the main head quarter of the (Sudanese People Liberation Army) SPLA. We arrived late in the afternoon and we found the town saturated with many thousands of SPLA, fighters.

Because of the political tension which exists between the two countries, the Sudanese government assists the Ethiopian oppositions at the south-west, while Ethiopia supports the SPLA fighters in the north-west.

Our pain and physical condition improving day by day sometimes we laugh, making jokes out of anything. The two drivers of Fiona and Marry namely, Tamiru and Yonnas, are very clever guys, finding smart and helpful ideas and encouraging the team when everything gets darker during the entire journey.

During bad times under those restrictions when we become sick, depressed, and when a glimpse of hope fades away, they have the talent to entertain and sing. They have the strength to create hope in our heart. I have to admire their selfless character.

Our head office of the AMSC camp was located just about three miles away from the town of Assossa. Many of people have already been informed prior to our arrival and many of our colleagues could not wait to see us who came to the town centre to welcome us, including those who escaped through the fences during the invasion at 'Sirba 1', Jarso.

Our close friends were shocked by our looks. Many of them gave us a big hug and shook our hands one by one with mixed emotions, at the first sight, their expression was filled with sadness, few of them cried in tears. Our condition speaks by itself and there was no need to tell anyone what we went through.

The AMSC had already shut down the operations in the entire region of Assossa, and we did not get to see most of the workers and colleagues. We found a few workers who remained at the camp to look after the farm machineries.

When we arrived at the camp, the manager, Mr Mulat, welcomed us and during the night a big party was thrown and our pain seemed to be pushed aside for a while.

Besides the work I do, I had good personal relationships with Mr Mulat and his families. On several occasions he advised me how to handle and deal with the social problems of the workers.

He was not a member of the ruling party, a man in his position commonly expected to be one of them, but he has no tendency of acquiring political power or did not want to be part of a distorted political system and that may have contributed, he was loved and respected by the workers and communities at large.

The party was over, and we began to think of our families. I was nervous and very desperate and restless to get to my family as everyone else. After a couple of days in Assossa, it was time to move again, back home.

The next morning a big gathering took place for the last prayer. In addition, we took pictures and exchanged addresses and discussed where we could meet again in future; our families lived thousands of miles apart.

We decided to meet in three months' time in the capital, Addis Ababa, at the head office of AMSC. For the moment, we all had the same thought in mind—to get to our families as soon as possible.

*   *   *

My family lives about two hundred miles away to the South from Addis. First I need to get to Addis before I travel to my birth place. Five days to our arrival in Assossa, I board a small domestic plane, in the afternoon, mid of August, from Assossa to Addis.

Two hours later, we arrived in Addis. I spend the night at the hotel, closer to the bus station, and the next morning, I board the bus and after eight hours of journey late in the afternoon, I was in my hometown Dilla.

I was born in a middle-class family; my mother died at a young age, and I was about two years old and did not get to know her. It was my father who took good care of my sisters and myself.

My two sisters, Zahra and Sittina, are older than I was, by two and three years respectively. I also had half-brothers and sisters, but we were not close to each other, not bonded, and drifted apart at an early age.

My father passed away in January 1981 at the age of eighty-five, and for us it was a great loss. He was very caring, kind, and loving person. He died of natural causes after a long illness.

We had a strong bond and a deep love for each other, when I was at Fashim in detention in those terrible conditions, I had a concern all the time, about my family and friends was and it was worrying me every single day.

Although it was difficult to ignore and forget the thought about my family, I had to find away to keep myself occupied and locked away my personal feelings to avoid more stress.

When I arrived at Dilla town, nobody was expecting me. My family had never been notified. When I get to my home, my two sisters screamed and cried. It was a moment of excitement.

Shortly, the neighbors and old friends of mine came over. The news spread very quickly. My house was filled with many people welcoming and wishing me good health.

My sisters did not get the news of the kidnapping until one week before our release. I thought to myself, 'It was a good thing that if they had never known at all. I do not want them to suffer because of me.'

They did not know the details how and why we were kidnapped, and by the time when I got home, they just heard of the news and getting prepared to go to Assossa in search of me.

My family never got to know what I went through. I did not want to open up. I kept everything sealed to myself. I loved my sisters dearly. I felt, it would be unfair on my behalf to reveal everything, which might cause them discomfort.

As the time went by, so many questions floating in my mind related to the past, I tried to avoid, however it bounces back affecting me in many ways. I need to talk; I need to tell someone; I need to be heard.

I became increasingly agitated, and the anger started to build up, week after week. The answers would be far away and difficult to find. I do not know if I will ever get answers. Why me? Why?

When I was sent to Jarso the first time, I had no information of the existence and activities of the rebel fighters or never been told formally as Jarso was a high security area. It was a time of rush, time for farming for the dying settlers.

The central government and it`s representatives did not concern about the safety of the workers. They do not want to hear problems, they scared away and punished anyone who even spreads information of the presence of the armed fighters.

At the time, I was given two jobs simultaneously, as workshop head and as administrator. I asked myself why they needed to do that. There are qualified people who could undertake the administration side of the job at Jarso.

They might have adequate information and are aware of the real danger, and cautiously might avoid working at Jarso. Why were the cadres kept silent about the security problems. They might think it would destabilise their operations.

Why was every information kept hidden from us? Who were they? Who needs protection and against who? These were some of the questions I was battling to get answers. Often I got depressed when I thought about it.

I could see some of the things clearly and many miles away from where I am sitting now that happened during and prior to the invasion at Jarso. At the time we had one thing in mind and nothing else, we were totally focused on the farming operation and completely unaware of the danger.

The cadres are responsible for running the operation of the entire settlement program. They knew about the rebel fighters and were fully aware of the danger and vacate the region few days prior to the invasion.

In one way or another, many of the secrets and information become revealed to us after we came back to Jarso and Assossa. It did help us to discover many things; however it re-freshens the anger as well.

The cadres and authorities failed every one of us, ignored the fundamental safety procedures, and abandoned the settlers and the communities at large. They were armed and responsible for the security and protection in all the settlement areas, beside their political propaganda.

I thought about many things that happened prior to the invasion. There were some significant indications, which we never noticed at the time, but when the dust settled and everything came to rest, I started to see some of the things clearly.

Just one week prior to the Jarso invasion, the leader of the cadre approached me at my small house. He was carrying two rifles, and I was wondering why he was carrying two when he needed only one.

After a short greetings he said, 'You need a rifle for your personal protection and here is one for you.' He handed over to me a rifle along with two small packets of ammunition, as if a birthday gift.

He did not explain why I need protection and against who? After all, we had many problems and differences with cadres, due to their interference in our day-to-day activities. They are not educated or professionals, but they have a political power to impose anything they wish.

We both knew we do not like each other. There has to be something, a hidden agenda. No one would give a rifle to someone without investigating who the person is or without signing any formal document.

I had no experience in handling any kind of firearm, and I do not like guns and he did not ask if I had any training. Instead he just said, 'Have a nice day', before he went out of the room. He was very quick and did not want to waste time trying to avoid further questions.

I was not very much concerned about the firearm, and personally, I had no enemies, but why is he concerned about me. The big question did not get off my mind. I decided to discuss this dilemma with my close friends, and slowly I pushed the rifle with the ammunition under my bed.

The following day, we heard many kinds of conflicting information about the sudden disappearance of those cadres from the scene. Later in the day, the rumors become real.

We had the confirmation: 'All the cadres vacate the settlement area.' But no one knows where and the cause. 'They packed everything and drove away with their Land Rover,' just a day before the invasion.

We thought they might be going to Nedjo town for shopping or meetings, but why do they need to pack everything? Moreover, why fifteen of them at the same time. We did not consider the move as a big issue and did not want to believe the idea of escape.

Political cadres are highly respected people because of their authoritarian tendency with enormous power given by the ruling party. Most of them are uneducated and depend on the weapon they carry, and not discussions, to find solutions.

Considering the behaviour of the cadres, we have concluded, they will fight to their death and will never abandon the people they stood for. And that made us less concerned. It was a big error, a misjudgement on our part.

After our return, we have learned the true story prior to the invasion; the rebels had distributed several pamphlets in the forest stating, 'All civilians should leave the area immediately'.

This information was kept away from the civilians and communities at large; it was unknown to us except the cadres and their close intelligence; they knew exactly what was to happen in a few days' time.

They packed and just left, without telling anyone. They may not want the farming operation disrupted, but they put us at risk, exposed us to danger, and did not care for the rest of civilians.

I tried to linkup all the information together trying to get a clear picture. Slowly I started to understand the mystery behind the confusion, but there is more to be revealed as time progresses.

I kept on asking why and how it happened. And the more I got deeper, it became clearer. It made me furious thinking about it all the time, and it affected me tremendously—not only myself, but my colleagues as well.

I started to attend a small clinic in my area, my head was shaking and when it does, I become restless, tense and sweaty. Sometimes I tried to forget everything and shift my thought to something else; however, when an innocent person suffers forcefully to an extreme, it is not easy to forget and not to think again.

When I calmed myself down, I felt better and that was the method I was told to practice. I got this problem five to six times a day. My condition improved the more I practiced and treated myself.

The state does not have a support system, and I belong to poor family. Due to variety of reasons, many young men and women are affected by mental illnesses. I think joblessness, poverty, and depression are the main factors.

I have deep thought and love for my colleagues, although I am not a medical professional on this matters, I would imagine it might require very long time to heal, especially from their emotional problems.

I believe it would be a better alternative if we got together to talk about the past. It would be easier to deal with our common problems collectively. We are the ones affected, and we understand our problems. I hope the appropriate time will arrive. One day we will be together.

Three months later in mid November 1988, I began to prepare myself to go to Addis, to our head office. My family did not like me to go, but I insisted it was time to go and find out about everything. Something pushed me from inside. I can't sit back and do nothing! But I knew there is nothing I can do.

Someone has to be held accountable and responsible for our suffering, but we all knew for the fact in Ethiopian politics and many African countries, accountability does not exist.

Most African leaders amend the constitution in their favor, whenever they need. All the power belonged to the leader, and most of them would like to keep the power beyond their lifetime, and pass it on to the next generation.

The rebel organisation operates not only in the forest, but also in towns and big cities as well, high government offices, and the business sectors. They have infiltrated almost in to every segment and activity throughout the country.

Through secret communications, a number of high government officials provide vital information and strategies to the fighters, commanding them from their offices, far away in the jungle, undetected.

It was not an easy task for the central government to distinguish the bad people among his own party leaders. It was so complicated. Moreover they sabotage and they mislead, spread distorted information against the state to create uncertainty in the nation.

I went to Addis to the head office of the AMSC, the first time since the Jarso kidnapping took place, and I met none of my colleagues. The office was filled with many employees, but I hardly recognised any of them.

We work in the farm hundreds of miles away. Previously, I had no visual contact with the guys at the head office; however, we do communicate every single day through the radio, reporting the farming progress and so on . . . We have already established good relationships previously. Now, when we see each other, we become good friends.

Tamiru and Yonnas report to their head office of the Irish concern. That is different from ours and is situated in a different location in the capital; I would assume they might be at their office for reporting after visiting their families.

The three settlers, Aseffa, Tilahun, and Seido, remain at Jarso with their families. They were not employees of the AMSC Irish concern and do not require to report. In Ethiopia, there is no support system for victims, and no counseling or rehabilitation program exist.

I heard Gecho has already reported and transferred to a small town called Gedeb. And this sight is one of AMSC branches in the central region. The AMSC expanding it's operation from the west to the central region of Ethiopia, which is relatively peaceful.

The AMSC is a sub division of the Min. of Agriculture, initially created to assist the settlers on farming activities at the west, which was abandoned due to the security problem.

Faisal is the youngest and the shortest of our member. He was a sportsman, an athlete. He has a kind of restless behaviour unable to stand or sit in one position. During our journey, we used to send him to collect firewood, fruit, or anything, and he was willing and happy to do anything. The pain in his leg was getting better before he left to his family.

Gecho and Haile, both of them are tall and thin, now they become even very thin, skinny and unrecognizable. During our journey, Gecho always stays next to me. He is emotional by nature, kind hearted, easily upset or cried. Gecho, is honest and real person and never pretend.

Although Haile is among us, we consider him as distant and an unknown person. He has an odd character. He doesn't like discussions or conversations with anyone on any matters. If he does, he keeps it very short and simple. Sometimes I use different methods to make him talk, but nothing could surprise him. He remains a gentle and very disciplined person.

We have developed a special bond, a lot of caring and sharing. Most of all, there is a great deal of trust among us. I believe we have conquered the most difficult journey in our lifetime, and through this process, we have developed unforgettable and lifetime relationships. We consider ourselves as one big family.

The authorities at the head office knew exactly what we went through and the brutality of the kidnappers but did not approach us formally or talked about the incident after our return and did not bother even to inform our families or friends, after the kidnapping took place.

Certainly there are members of political activists who are educated who held high positions in government offices, trained at Fashim or any other locations who are members of the rebel fighters, who supply information's and provide logistical support. We do not know them, we may have reported back to these ghosts.

In a volatile country where political storm exists, many things do happen secretly. I have witnessed families who split into two groups, supporting different factions or political groups, and people who abandoned their families for the sake of politics. It does not end there; many thousands sacrificed their life for what they stood for and believed in, whether for wrong reason or not.

There is no question in mind, what happened to us is happening everyday in different parts of Ethiopia, either by the fascist government or different rebel groups. We left ignored by the officials. They had shown no remorse. On the other hand, no one dared to comment or criticise openly the activities of political factions.

I found none of my colleagues of the Fashim. I thought they might have already reported and most probably allocated to different places. To find out I need to see someone who holds a higher rank in the office.

The administrator is a matured and bureaucratic man, he has good knowledge and understanding of the rebel fighters and their demands, but did not want to comment or take my concern seriously or did not want to hear anything of the rebel fighters. Initially that was not my intention to make him understand.

He told me, 'Your colleagues have already been reported and assigned to different locations and you also have to undertake as a technical trainer at a place called Chagni, located at the remote semi-desert, northern part of Ethiopia.'

*   *   *

Salini is an Italian contractor who is running a rural development project in the northern part of Ethiopia. Part of the program was to cultivate land for the settlers.

In order to run their project, they need skilled work force. They need to train tractor operators in order to plough the land. Salini project requires technical assistance and that was how the AMSC engaged with Salini.

Two of us were assigned to carry out the training program—myself and Mr Atnafu, the technical director at AMSC head office. He was a leader of the two-men group.

For three months, we provided technical training, for sixty-five young farmers who were recruited from the surrounding farming areas. Theoretical lessons were given in the classroom and practical lessons given on the field.

We presented the teachings in a simplified and easy way for the learners to understand. The main objective was to replace the old traditional farming method with new technology.

They need to acquire technical knowledge in order to operate and use farming machineries when ploughing, and to carry out the daily maintenance on tractors and attachments of farm machineries in general.

Three months would be a short period of time to gain adequate knowledge of the techniques; however, the subject was focused mainly on the operational side of the machines in conjunction with the safety procedures.

It was my first time to teach. I found it interesting, satisfying, and enjoyable. I do the teachings seven long hours a day, including weekends. The interaction between the students was marvelous. It was one of my first time giving knowledge to others. Most of all, it was the best remedy to ease emotional problems.

Healing is a process, it would take longer time to get rid of the trauma associated with the past, I have to find a way to adjust myself accordingly and focus more in daily duties than thinking of the past. However, there was a time when the past comes at the front.

By the end of February 1989, the three-month training had been completed. We began to prepare to go back to our head office in Addis, and couple of days before we left, we heard the good news—all the graduates had become the new employees of the contractor Salini, as tractor operators.

That was the happiest moment in my life. I felt I am worthy of something. I can make a difference in other people's life. It was my first experience in teaching, to give knowledge to someone.

When I got to Addis, the following day I went to our head office, trying to meet my colleagues, with whom I had no contact for the last three months. One of the problems in Ethiopia is communication, especially when you go to the remote areas; you should know you are out of reach.

However, none of my colleagues were available at the head office, but I found out, they had already been assigned to different sites of AMSC branches within the central region not far from Addis.

*   *   *

One week later, I was transferred to one of the AMSC site, which is called Gedeb, located at the eastern part of the central region of Ethiopia, not far from Addis, about 100 miles away.

On my way to Gedeb, I was hoping that at least I would be able to find one of my colleagues, who were kidnapped previously from Jarso. It was the second week of March 1989.

Gedeb was a dusty and windy small town surrounded by big state farms. The town was saturated with farm workers. The people in Gedeb are likely to be more civilised than those in Jarso, probably because of the influence of the surrounding big cities such as Nazareth, Debrezeit, and Shashemene.

The AMSC camp was about a mile away from the town center. The next day I went to the office of the administration to report, and I met a man, whom I did not expect to see. Probably I forgot everything about him and began to wonder who I could see next.

Mr Tesfaye was the manager at Megelle, AMSC site, few miles away from Assossa. That was my first experience working at the settlement area before I left to Germany. He was very strict concerning the performance of each worker. Moreover, he managed the attendance regularly.

Since then, he had been transferred to several sites of AMSC, before he was allocated to Gedeb as a manager. I was surprised; I did not expect to see him. The last time I met him at Megelle was in 1987.

Shortly I met Gecho. I was very glad to see him. Physically he looked good, but he had emotional problems, difficulties with socialising with people. He was the only one among us, who transferred to Gedeb.

He told me he has difficulties of aggressiveness, talking alone, depression, and anger. As I understood, these are the symptoms of the previous illness, which started just before we moved out of Fashim. When I met him, he was under constant medical observation in Gedeb.

Most of the workers understood what he went through and the state of his illness, and supported him in every possible way. However, as time went by his condition deteriorated.

The AMSC site at Gedeb was more advanced and organised than that of Jarso. Most of all, it was peaceful and there was no any concern about rebel movement or kidnapping.

Gecho and myself remain very close friends. We discussed the past and the future. I could understand Gecho more than anyone else. We had no problem of communication. He approached me differently from the rest of the workers at Gedeb.

Gecho was very disciplined and gentle. He was likable; often he gets angry, and when he does, he became extremely violent and outrageous and when he become sober, he could not be able to remember what he has done wrong short while ago.

Gradually, I associated myself with everyone and the job, unlike Assossa here in Gedeb the operation is done strictly for commercial purposes based on profit, as there are no settlers and private individuals who own the land.

The farmers should pay for every service they could get. Starting from clearing of the land, plaguing, cultivation, harvesting, or any services they may require. Prior to the operation, strictly each farmer should make the payment in advance.

About three months later, and one morning as I was busy at the workshop I heard someone talking to me, the sound came closely from behind, suddenly I put down the tools I was holding and slowly got up from my seat, because I knew that voice very well.

When I turn slowly, it was him Tolossa standing in front of me. For a while I remain speechless looking to his eyes with disbelief. I never imagined, not even in my wildest dreams, to see Tolossa again.

He greeted me very politely and shook my hand, but I showed no interest in talking to him or greet him back. I think he understood my reaction. He gained more weight and looked absolutely healthy.

Tolossa was the man who betrayed us at bad times, who sold us out to the kidnappers and who spied on us; he was the informer while we were at the Fashim camp in Sudan at the hands of the rebel fighters.

It was the first time I met him since they took him away from our small hut at Fashim detention center. Difficult to forget what he has done to us. At that time every one of us was disappointed and angered by his actions.

He just arrived here at Gedeb, AMSC branch as a junior mechanic. Our head office do not consider employee's political agenda or their backgrounds as long as they perform their duty properly and accept all the rules and regulations required by the AMSC.

The first thing click to my mind was, he must have been sent for different Reasons, probably as an agent, he may have an assignment or a mission to spy, he may have contacts here in Gedeb. I have to think carefully in order to get a clear picture.

There must be something sinister, secrecy unknown to us. The disappearance and appearance of Tolossa, in both occasions, it happened suddenly, but the people around me have no idea, except the fact, he was kidnapped by the rebel fighters and escaped and made it to his country. We knew Tolossa differently, a traitor a sabotage.

A week later Gecho and myself decided to approach him for serious talks. One morning we went to a small hotel where he stayed. We needed to iron out straight some of the things affecting us.

Immediately we started firing questions how he managed to come out from there, as it was impossible for anyone to make it through the forest alone. 'Where did they take you that morning along with Tilahun?' In addition, 'Why did they keep you behind leaving Tilahun?' 'Why did you spy on us?' We asked him direct and confrontational questions.

He became very embarrassed and ashamed, but we kept silent to listen to what he had to say. We clearly indicated to him, we needed serious explanations; he understood, we cannot let him go away easily.

He tried to avoid eye contact, looking to different direction, fighting with himself with enormous guilt, searching for excuses, but it was real and we stood firm The only option left for him was to tell us the whole truth and nothing else.

Slowly he admits he was wrong and apologises for what he has done to us, but he did not want to give us any details for the rest of the questions and became completely silent.

We kept asking ourselves, why do they kidnapped us, and why do we need to face all the suffering what was the reason for our release and what happened to the two women, Fiona and Marry.

Tolossa, did not want to give us direct answers and refused to answer any further questions related to his secret activity with the rebel fighters and that was a disappointment on our side. However, before we moved out, we let him know, we will not accept his apology until we get complete answers.

The rebels secretly operated in big cities, towns, and villages. We strongly suspect, Tolossa could be one of the new recruit. We just do not want to be trapped again; we want a normal life and do not want anyone to follow us secretly, the state agent or the rebel fighters.

Tolossa belongs to the tribe of those fighters, born and grown up in Wollega province at the western part of Ethiopia, where Jarso is located and a high concentration of the tribe exist. He was about twenty-four years old. He was very private, silent, and an introverted person who kept everything to himself.

At the end of July 1989, Gecho became very sick of mental illnesses, and his condition deteriorated dramatically. He could not control himself. He had to leave and attend the mental hospital in the capital Addis.

He had severe depression, unable to think and perform his job properly, loss of appetite, memories and most of all he could not control his outrageous anger. He becomes a dangerous person to himself and for the people around him as well.

After Gecho was long gone, I occasionally I become loneness and often depressed. I missed someone very important in my life. We have developed a great deal of trust and true brotherhood proven through despicable hardships.

Particularly, Gecho and I have many things in common however, nothing is more important than his health. He requires proper and urgent medical attention.

Gradually Tolossa, becomes known as a traitor by our workers and some of the people in the town as well, the implication lead him to be rejected and unwanted by some of the people. He remains out of work in his small room alone and depressed.

During his stay in Gedeb, we have observed closely his activity, if he had any contacts related to the rebel fighters at work or outside of the working environment, but we found no trace of such activity.

Presumably, many people do not agree with the concept of tribalism. It is used as a tool to cultivate many young people to join and fight the dirty war. Tribalism was the main objective and driving power of the rebel fighters to gain their independent.

Tolossa during his absence from work none of our workers tempted to visit him. On several occasion I paid a visit trying to talk to him in a different tune. I knew the enormous burden of guilt he carries.

In every visit I made he did not want to divulge or has shown no interest to mention about the fighters or how he managed to free himself. He may have concerns of the repercussions, he has decided to keep the secrets to himself, and die with it.

The last time when I went to his house, I found him laying on his bed. He looked at me with discomfort and confronted with the reality, beginning to understand the mistakes he has done.

I could feel the expressions on his face, a combination of fear and guilt, as tears poured from his eyes, I have understood his conditions, he needs urgent attention.

He was under big pressure, from the workers and the surrounding people's, at the time many kinds of rumors flying around, a 'traitor', he works for the enemy, so and so forth' for that reason, he was isolated, and had a big social problem.

After long silence, he requested a transfer to another branch. That was the only words he spoke to me, before I left his room. I could feel, he was not happy with my presence; there was a sense of discomfort.

One week later, I have made the arrangements to transfer him, but before he gets the good news his health conditions deteriorated rapidly, he has gone and disappeared from the scene without a trace and that was the last time I heard about Tolossa.

As time goes by everything seems to be fade away about the two colleagues of mine, who went in different directions. Gecho and Tolossa, it was not easy to forget two of my friends, a good friend who went to the Hospital and the bad one who went missing.

I was determined to find the rest of my colleagues, where they might have gone, victims of the terrible tragedy, as there were no established support system who deals in such matters.

At the end of November, I heard the bad news Haile and Feisal dismissed from the AMSC for not reporting on a given time to their locations as the policy of the department.

I used to be more comfortable to talk to my friends who suffered with me, Who I share ideas, since they gone, there was nobody to talk to, I prefer to Keep my thought to myself.

*   *   *

In the beginning of December, I took a short leave for a family visit. There was something building in my mind for a long time, but I needed to consult my family first.

Since I came to Gedeb and since I had no contact with my colleagues, I started to lose appetite for a job gradually. I developed a feeling of not being free and felt controlled by someone unseen.

Something pushing me from inside to leave my job and go far away to free myself, where nobody can recognise me, where I could be free from the past, from everything.

I went to Dilla where my family lives, the town where I was born. I need to convince my sisters that I need to leave my country. I need their blessings and support, but most of all their permission.

It was the time when political tension got to the highest peak, a time of war, total unrest with many restrictions, many political factions pushing very hard to throw the fascist regime of Mengistu.

My family was fully aware and understood the political condition on the ground and did understand my personal ambition, on why I decided to leave. At first, they were reluctant. After analysing the situation, they accepted my decisions to leave the country.

My main intention was to go to Kenya and find a suitable job, to assist my family back at home financially and lead a stable and peaceful life without stress, to get away, to free myself.

There was someone in Kenya. I knew this person from the childhood, a distant family, a businessperson who had been leaving in Nairobi for many years by the name of Isaac known by his nickname, Marata. And that was my destination.

Kenya is a neighboring country at the south, a destination for thousands of Ethiopian, Sudanese, and Somalian refugees who fled their country for many reasons and many of them lived their permanently doing business and different kinds of jobs.

A week later, I went to Addis to our head office probably for the last time to submit my resignation letter. In December 1990, I resigned officially from AMSC, and that was final.

Psychologically I felt better since I resigned from my job, as if a big burden had been taken off my shoulders. One week later, I received a letter indicating I am cleared of all my duties and it was time to prepare for the long journey to Nairobi, Kenya.

Before I began my journey, I needed to find my colleagues. Unfortunately, I was not lucky enough to meet any of them. I would assume they must have been down and depressed, battling with unemployment and poverty, leaving with their families.

Due to security reasons, there had been restrictions of movement, and the problem of transportation was the main obstacle to reach from one point to another. They lived deep in the rural areas in different parts of the country.

One Way to the South

One morning in February 1991, I began the first leg of the journey. I boarded a bus from Addis to the small border town, which lay between Ethiopia and Kenya called Moyalle.

I had no legal travel documents, and two days later, I crossed to the Kenyan border with hundreds of people without difficulty. At the time, I was not concerned about legality or the risk of crossing the borders illegally. It was a mass exodus driven from Ethiopia due to the political tension.

I reported to the Kenyan officials as an asylum seeker, at the sister town of Moyalle over the borderline in Kenya. The next morning, I was told to join a group of Ethiopian refugees a couple of miles further out of town, in a place called Hoha.

I had to adapt and adjust myself with the new situation and environment very quickly at Hoha. There was no turning back, and I had to look forward to meeting new people, new places, and new environment.

A week later the number of refugees increased sharply and the United Nations officials had decided to move us away from the border zone to a proper settlement area, deep in Kenyan territory to a place called Walda.

Walda is about 50 miles in the Kenyan territory, extremely remote and a dry desert. There was no village or sign of life. There was no place or shelter to hide from the blazing sun.

The food items had been distributed by the UNHCR. Everyone was given a tent as a means of shelter. One week later Walda had been transformed as a formal settlement area.

Walda was guarded and strictly protected by the Kenyan security forces for any possible escape or movement of the refugees to the central region of Kenya. As the number of refugees increased, the living conditions deteriorated rapidly.

There was no proper sanitation. The spread of diseases became a major concern. Some of the people developed symptoms of vomiting, diarrhoea and fever. Children were the ones who were affected the most.

Each tent accommodated four people. I was living with two Ethiopians—Daniel and Abraham—and one Eritrean guy, Josef. Previously, none of us knew each other, it was the small tent that brought us together.

Gradually we started talking and developed good relationships. It was common and natural as people got together to talk to each other and express their feelings in different ways as a means of communication.

They told me part of their stories as politics drove them out of their country. The two Ethiopians were engineers. And the Eritrean guy came from the medical profession. I listened their stories day after day, but I was cautious, and did not want to tell my personal story in depth.

Two weeks later the number of refugees increased by more than half and the small camp became saturated and life became unbearable. We could not stand the harsh environment. Four of us decided to take a risk, to move out and walk on foot and free ourselves, to go far away to the central region, to the big town of Mersabit.

Mersabit lay about 100 miles ahead to the south, about 200 miles before Nairobi, the capital of Kenya, but the trend was not as easy as it looked. It contained many dangerous elements; there were many risks.

Through my previous experience, I always had a feeling that I could travel any distance any time, but this time it was so different—hostile weather, wilderness, and dry desert. Moreover it was a foreign country.

On my stay at Walda, I met different kinds of people, and one of them was young looking and a very polite person, who was from my hometown Dilla, by the name of Meskerem.

When we decided to escape, he was part of the team, but he became sick just one day prior to our departure. He became sick of malaria. Meskerem was fully aware of the danger and the obstacles on the way ahead. He would not be able to cross the desert on foot and decided to stay at Walda.

Meskerem lived in one of the tent opposite ours. We went to his tent to say goodbye. At the time he was very sick and could not get up. We kept everything secret and no one should know about the trip. The security forces strictly monitor and do not allow any movement out of the camp; there was a penalty for those who were found to be escaping.

*   *   *

Day One

On the early morning of Saturday we got up before sunrise. We packed only that we needed most for the journey. Canned food and water. The rest of our belongings had to be sealed and thrown away.

We closed our tent and walked away slowly following one another in short distances. Several tents were lined up in both sides occupied by the refugees from the Sudan and Ethiopian.

We slipped out of the camp silently unnoticed. We walked through the bush parallel to the dusty road, to avoid any exposure as security forces were regularly patrolling the road.

At the same time we had to look out for the bandits and wild animals in the bush. Cautiously we walked throughout the day between the thorny trees and sharp stones in the blazing sun.

We walked very fast for the first five hours and slowed down as we moved deeper into the stretched rocky fields. We came across skeletons of wild animals scattered, as the sign of draught.

Unlike the root to Fashim, the journey from Walda to Mersabit was relatively peaceful. We cruised through the dry desert by our own, under no captivity or constant intimidations.

We walked throughout the day with short rests now and then. At the end of the day and before the sun disappeared, we moved to the higher ground to spend the night.

We did not make much progress in our journey compared to the distance we should have been covering. The two guys, Daniel and Abraham, had a feeling of regret and uncertainty they had made a bad decision, but Josef had shown his determination to complete the mission.

I had previous experience of walking great distances. It was not really a big concern on my part, but my new friends had a doubt at the beginning and that was not a good start. I tried my best to encourage them and simplify.

It was a calm and peaceful night. The shadows of the mountains were visible as we lay down on the ground. And suddenly we heard the sound of a vehicle from the distance heading to Marsabit. That was the first truck; we did not get to see any kind of vehicle throughout the day.

It may probably have been the army truck. We did not know. We kept our distance and avoided any exposure. There were risks. If they found us, we would be considered as escapees and definitely be arrested and sent back to Walda. We did not want that to happen.

At nightfall, we could hear the sounds of different wild animals from the distance, sometimes very close to us; the desert seemed to be as dangerous as the forest. We gathered a few information before we started the journey.

We heard of the danger, venomous snakes, desert lions, and the bandits, but we were determined to get out of Walda because of the spread of diseases, shortage of food, and the crowd.

There had been a sharp increase in the number of people who were affected by malaria and other diseases. The medical facilities were not capable of handling the flux of people. We decided to escape and not be deterred by fear.

Josef and I were sitting and talking most of the night as the two guys were fast asleep covering their faces with their jackets. I had a sense of relief not to have Meskerem with us.

*   *   *

Day Two

Geographically the area was located in the equatorial region and the weather was quite different—very hot with heavy sunstroke during the day and it became very cold at nightfall.

Early in the morning, we decided to follow the dusty road before the sun got hot, and when we heard the sound of vehicles, we moved quickly and hid in the bush.

As the going got tough through the hot sun, we threw away some of our belongings—our jackets and jersey, and some of the things which were not very important—to ease the burden.

As we walked through the bush, we came across a dozen of ostrich eggs; we carried some of them along as a source of food. We did not know what lay ahead of us. Our main concern was water, and we had no water left.

Since the previous night, we had seen only three vehicles moving in the same direction at different times; that was worrying. Gradually, we became dehydrated. It was impossible to walk specially during the day and there was no river or any other sign of water.

When we began our journey, we hoped we would be able to get a lift, a free ride, but fear of breaking the rules kept us away from the main road, but now we decided to walk in the middle of the road, to be seen by anyone, including the army. We had run out of everything.

It was our second day. Early in the afternoon as we rested under the shade of the Acacia tree, we heard the sound of a truck, and suddenly we sprung from where we sat to get a glimpse of the truck.

We stood in the middle of the road; we could see the white truck from afar, followed by a swirling of dust, coming from north, heading to the south, probably to the capital, Nairobi. The police vehicles were identifiable. They were dark green in colour and that was not one of them.

As he came closer, the driver pulled the truck to one side of the road and called out at us angrily, 'Are you crazy! You need to go back. The bandits will kill you. Even if they don't, you will die of hunger.' He was telling us the truth; there wasn't even firewood. The stretched field and the mountains were covered with stones.

He noticed our physical condition and understood as we escaped from the Walda camp. We begged him to take us to Mersabit. It was an offence for any driver to transport asylum seekers from one point to another without authorisation.

After he consulted with one of his passengers kindly he said, 'Climb up quickly,' we climbed at the back of the truck as he spoke. Shortly, he handed us over a jar of water through the window. When we got something, we were tempted for something else. Just like a chain, our needs never ended. We needed food, and when we got something to eat, we started craving for a cigarette . . .

Just before sunset, he stopped somewhere between the rocky mountains and told us to step down. He showed us pointing his fingers towards the direction we should be going, a short cut, to Mersabit.

About an hour later, when we got to the mountain, the streetlight of Mersabit was visible from a short distance. It was nearly dark, and as we walked down, we came across a big house standing alone at the roadside.

When we got closer, we noticed it was a church; we stepped in hoping to get assistance. The little boy who noticed our presence informed the man who was sitting at the back of the church.

We looked terrible, covered with dust from head to toe; shortly, the old man came through. Immediately he understood. 'I knew you are escapees from Walda.' We said yes, by shaking our heads.

We needed water to wash, food, and a place to sleep. He was godly and a kind person. He did not want to question and was fully cooperative. He gave us everything we asked for. He was very pleased when we gave him the ostrich eggs.

Early in the morning, the old man gave us his advice. 'You need to get to the camp and register before the police came out on the street. Those who were not registered were always sent back to Walda with penalties.'

The windy and dusty town of Mersabit was found in the northern region of Kenya, the biggest town we came across, since we entered the Kenyan territory, a highly populated business town.

The Mersabit refugee center is one of the biggest in Kenya, run by the United Nations. So many Ethiopians, Somalians, Eritreans, and the Sudanese live at the camp.

The camp was guarded by the security force to make sure no one escapes to Nairobi or anywhere else, but we went in, through the main gate without difficulty. They usually controlled those who tried to escape from the camp and not the newcomers.

On our arrival, we submitted the applications as a political asylum at the office of the UNHCR. We were then provided with blankets and food parcels and allocated to one of the tents provided for refugees.

As we moved in, the Eritrean guy, Joseph, met his long-time friend and went with him to his tent, not far from ours. Three of us lived together in one big tent recently evacuated.

I had to adapt myself to the harsh environment, but it was difficult to deal with different kinds of people and different characters, and most of all, the rising temperature during the day was unbearable.

Two weeks later, three of us became good friends based on trust and loyalty. We started planning to move out again, to Nairobi, to the capital; our brain never settled.

I had the address of someone, a distant family, a successful businessperson, in Nairobi. I needed to contact him There was a good possibility he might rescue all three of us.

Mr. Isaac usually called by his nickname, Marata, meaning, crazy. By late 1970s, he abandoned his family and fled to Kenya. I am sure it was not for political reasons, it must have been for something else, which I did not know.

I was not sure if he would remember me. I had no interactions with Isaac during those days. I made the first move, a call to Nairobi, to his house. It was Isaac who picked up the phone. Nairobi was about two hundred miles away from Mersabit.

After a long conversation, he told me someone would pick me up within a week, a truck driver by the name of Suleiman, but Isaac was not ready to assist the rest of my friends.

I was not happy to leave my dear friends, Daniel and Abraham, behind, but they insisted I should go ahead with the arrangements; there would be time where we could get together again.

One week later, I met the truck driver, Suleiman. He told me at nightfall, I should get out of the camp, and wait for him at the main road, out of town. I asked him if he is willing to take us all together, but Suleiman refused. Due to the risks involved, he did not want to assist more than one person at a time.

Daniel, Abraham, and I went together out of town, where we could meet Suleiman. At that moment Joseph was not with us. He already made his own arrangement with his friends. We suspect they also have decided to escape at a different time.

I said goodbye to my friends and climbed up at the back of the big truck and slipped into the hiding place. Three days later and after so many roadblocks, the morning of Saturday, 13 April 1991, we arrived at Nairobi, the capital of Kenya.

*   *   *

Nairobi (Kenya)

Mr Isaac lived in the center of the city in small house with his two daughters and two sons. He ran his own business, hiring of trucks, for delivering goods, and gradually I became part of the family, but that was the hardest part.

His four kids born in Ethiopia and brought up in Kenya have adopted different cultures and behaviour. As a new arrival, I found it very difficult to associate myself with the family.

A few weeks later, I was told the bad news—the instant death of my older sister Zahra, back in Ethiopia. I was terribly shocked and went crazy. I found it very difficult to accept the loss of my beloved sister.

I loved my sister so much. I mourned for weeks, depressed, and did not want to accept the reality. My head started shaking. I became restless and could not sleep at night. I felt guilty, lonely, and miserable.

Nearly for two months, I stayed by myself alone. I avoided any contacts with some of the people I knew. Gradually, I began to realise, I cannot stay away from friends and everything. Eventually, I started communicating and socialising with the people around me.

Isaac offered me a job to keep me busy and to get me out of the sadness. He was aware how deeply I was affected by the death of my sister Zahra. I became a coordinator for the trucking operation.

Nairobi is one of the big cities in East Africa. The footmarks of colonial power still exists. Banks, big insurance companies and other institutions in the economic sector are controlled and run by the whites, who benefited from the previous colonial regime.

The margin between the rich and the poor seems to be very big. Kenya is somehow civilised and democratic, which is more of a Western influence. However, corruption and crime are the main challenges. At the time Kenya was one of the most corrupt country.

Mr Isaac has a small number of old trucks. He operates as a sub-contractor to deliver food items and different materials specifically to different refugee centers across the country and beyond, to the Sudan in the west and to the Somalian border in the east.

My main task was to organise and regulate the trucking operation. Wherever and whenever goods need to be transported, I would be contacting the senders and facilitate the process.

While I stayed in Kenya, I did not have any legal document. I had applied at the Ethiopian embassy in Nairobi, and one month later, I was, given the Ethiopian passport.

During this period, political change took place in Ethiopia. A political party called the Ethiopian People's Revolutionary Democratic Front (EPRDF) seized the capital, and the military regime was finally toppled by a coalition of armed forces in 1991.

Shortly, Ethiopia accepted and recognised Eritrea as an independent state. It was a time of change, a new beginning, a new political arena, and the Eritreans who lived in Ethiopia found their way back home.

Ethiopia is Africa's oldest independent and one of the poorest states in the world. However, the country is also well known for its rich culture and diversity; the history of ancient Abyssinia goes back thousands of years.

Six months later, I gained more experience and associated myself with the environment and the job in Kenya, and everything looked promising, but not as it looked.

Mr Isaac, a successful Ethiopian businessperson, mainly known of his extreme violent and aggressive character, was much feared by his family and neighbors as well. He has a positive side—he was famous for his generosity, especially towards the poor and the needy.

The trucks usually travel long distances supplying different kinds of goods within and outside of the borders, sometimes it took us several days when we go to the Sudan, via Uganda to Nimble in Sudan, the territory of SPLA (Sudanese People liberation army).

There was no free time and constantly I was on the road, there was no time to do my personal things. The job I do was not convenient, however it was not about convenience, but I had no other options.

One year later, I heard about my three friends, and their whereabouts, whom I met at the border and travelled with me from Walda to Mersabit—Daniel, Abraham, and Josef.

I went to one of the biggest and the oldest refugee center in East Africa, Thika refugee camp. It is located in the outskirts of Nairobi, and recently many refugees, who were at Mersabit, have been transferred to this center.

It was about over one year since we become separated, when I met them at Thika, they were about to have an interview for screening among so many refugees who have been offered re-settlement at the USA.

I stayed in Kenya for the duration of three years and I was successful to speak the language, Swahili and adopt the culture, tradition and the way of life in Kenya, which is completely different from the country of my origin, Ethiopia.

All of these was about to change due to something that happened unexpectedly on Tuesday, 8 February 1994, which took me back to the drawing board, but I do not know why such things happen to me.

*   *   *

Our task was to deliver one big water tank to the UNHCR office located at the eastern side of Kenya, at the border town of Madera, about 500 miles away from Nairobi on the borderline between Kenya, Somalia, and Ethiopia. The driver of the truck was a person named Abdullah.

We drove from Nairobi late in the afternoon. We reached the small town called Garissa, about 200 miles before Madera. It was dark, and we decided to spend the night at Garissa town.

Unusually, the town was saturated with many trucks parked everywhere. We suspected there must have been something wrong, or something might have happened recently, but we did not bother as such.

The big news was all about the bandits who ambushed out of town on the way to the border. That was the reason the trucks were stranded. It was common in Kenya. Bandits were everywhere, especially on the borders.

The next day, early in the morning, we started our journey through the sandy unmarked road towards the Somalia border, ignoring the warnings, as false alarms do happen from time to time.

About thirty miles in our journey, suddenly the driver stopped in a matter of urgency staring towards the direction of the roadside, from his expression I noticed something was terribly wrong.

Seven of them, very young Somalians, were pointing their long rifle in the direction of the driver, shouting 'Stop! Stop!' The driver quickly stopped and switched off the engine.

They came closer to the truck, cautiously without losing their sight of us. They ordered, 'Put both your hands over your head and step outside.' We did as they said.

They dragged us to the side of the road, and they ordered, 'You must kneel down on the ground quickly.' We did as they wished; their character reminded me of those kidnappers at Jarso, and the rifle they carried was exactly the same as the rifle which was taken from the two old men, 'the bee hunters', during our journey from Jarso to Fashim.

I am not afraid of robbers or bandits. I was very sure they were looking for money; certainly it was not a matter of politics. As we kneeled down they asked, 'Where is the money? Put down all your possessions now.'

The previous night, when we heard about the situation, I did not ignore the information entirely; I hid the money in the roof of the cabin, which was for fuel, tollgates, and other purposes.

They took all our wallets, watches, and other personal items and went in to the cabin searching for any valuable materials. They threw out everything, but they could not get the money.

If they had found the money, I could probably be subjected to torture, because I had denied having any money. On the other hand if I had given them some, they would have demanded for more.

The driver is half Somalian and half Kenyan. He advised me how to react in such cases, I have adequate information's about the bandits and how they operate long before our journey. He speaks Somalian language fluently. He was very confident that no one would touch him and did not even moved out of the cabin.

One of the bandits came close to me and asked in broken English, 'What nationality are you?' I replied quickly, 'I am an Eritrean.' That was what I was told to say.

He said, 'Get up, you are free!' I did not understand the friendship of Somalia with Eritrea and that was not my concern.

They shifted their focus to the two Kenyans. They undressed them completely and beat them with a stick, until they bled and their fingers broke. The two black Kenyans cried for mercy, but no one tried to save them.

Abdullah was very relaxed and confident that nothing would happen to him. He was talking to the bandits, while they undressed and beat the two Kenyans. He did not try to save them; I think he was talking about something irrelevant.

An hour later, they told us to go; we then quickly climbed to our truck and drove away. The two naked Kenyans were still bleeding and shivering and so confused; they did not understand why they were treated differently from the rest of us.

I tried to calm them down and gave them old clothes of mine. And the driver gave them old shoes and painkiller tablets to ease the pain. The bandits do not like Kenyans, but I do not know why. And Abdullah did not want to speculate on these matters.

After we drove for about 20 miles, we stopped and got out of the truck to assess the damage. The two innocent Kenyans were still in a state of shock, analysing their battered bodies and wondering things could happen very quickly and unexpectedly.

There were no vehicles moving in both directions, and that was not the first time, and such incidents do happen from time to time in many parts of the Kenyan region.

I checked for the money and it was still safe and hidden in the secure place. I was sure no one would be able to find it easily. Shortly, we started moving again, hoping there were no more bandits ahead.

Simbire is a name given to that specific area where the tragedy took place. It was remote, and there was no indication previously if there was a village or human activity at all; it was dry sandy desert.

We drove through the night. There was no specific place or time to stop. We stopped only whenever we needed to make food and eat. We carried food items, gas stoves, and the necessary materials for making the food.

During the night, often we stopped when we were not sure of the direction, as it was sandy road. The tracks disappeared as the wind blew and that was where we stopped for a break.

After three days of journey, late in the afternoon we reached the border town of Madera, which connects the three neighboring countries, Ethiopia, Kenya, and Somalia.

An Australian-born gentleman, the head of the office at the UNHCR, welcomed us warmly. He felt terribly sorry of what we went through and promised he would provide any assistance we may require.

We appreciated his concern, but for the rest of the people around Madera, it seemed to be just a normal thing. Hijacking and kidnappings do happen from time to time. I think unemployment, poverty, and politics are the causes for criminal activities.

He was born and raised in a civilised and rich country, where human rights are respected and rules have to be followed, but here is Africa, where there is very little concern for human life.

Many people in the region are poor and subjected to live in difficult and harsh conditions. The killings, robberies, and lawlessness are daily occurrences. The more you go from the central region to the borders you carry the most risks.

Two days later, we recovered quickly, and it was time to leave. It would be a very long and boring journey and many things to be worried about, the robbers, the truck might break down . . . .

We have to make a move, we would be required for another trip and that was the bottom line. Six days later, we reached to Nairobi, because of the rain and muddy roads we were forced to slow down.

I reported the matter to the owner Mr Isaac, concerning the incident, which Happened at Simbire. He was not very surprised by the incident as it occurs from time to time, but for me it was a wake-up call.

Since it was part of my job to travel with the trucks from place to place, I become less interested doing this kind of job and the risk attached to it was much more than the benefit I could get out of it.

It was time for me to reconsider my options, and I had an idea, but I needed more information. I did not have a family or reliable friends for offering advice, but I had to make a decision without delay.

I have three options: to stay in Kenya and find a better job or return back to my country Ethiopia or to go ahead somewhere else, to a different country.I have to consider carefully before I made the final decision.

The first option to stay here—not possible due to the visa requirement. Since I do not have a work permit, it was difficult to extend my visas from time to time and that option falls away.

To go back to my country was not easy either. I lost my job before I came to Kenya, and there was very little chance of getting a new job, and there was still political unrest.

The remaining option was to go ahead to a different country. The question was where do I go from here? I need to consult someone I knew, a friend in Nairobi. We are not close friends, but he was just a friend to spend time and share information.

His name was Jamal, the son-in-law of Isaac, an Ethiopian national who came to Kenya so many years ago who pretended and considered himself as a Kenyan citizen, who did not have interest and forgot everything about his birth country, Ethiopia.

He advised me and promised for any assistance I may require. He insisted to go ahead for a better job that suited my qualification to South Africa or anywhere else, possibly out of Africa, than waste my time with Isaac. I then decided to go to South Africa.

Soon the momentum picked up, and I started gathering information about South Africa. At the same time, I informed my decision to my family back in Ethiopia, but I did not want to inform Mr. Isaac about my plans. I knew his negative reactions.

He wanted me to look after his own business, his own profit; I did not have specific salary or benefits. I was regarded as part of the family as an excuse for exploitation, and I felt that was unfair.

After I setup my mind, I went to Thika refugee camp to visit my colleagues to find out the progress of their resettlement program, but I was told, the program has been suspended due to unknown reasons. Daniel had been transferred to a different refugee centre, and the rest of them went back to Ethiopia.

Daniel, Abraham, and Joseph were good friends. We went through difficult times. We developed good friendship in a short space of time, but now they had gone, vanished, and since then I did not get to see any of them.

I felt sad for a while, but that was part of life. There is no guarantee. Changes come beyond our control. I was in detention at Fashim. I was thinking and praying just to get out of Fashim to save my life, but now I am planning to see the world for a better opportunity.

I have to think for myself, three years in Kenya, too much time without change. I need to make a move, I need to get away from Mr. Isaac and the family.

Destination South Africa

On 12 March 1994, I started the long journey to South Africa. First I went to the Tanzanian border town called Namanga. I got my entry visa, and the next day I travelled by bus to the capital city, Dar el salam.

Two days later, I crossed to Zambia border. I stayed at the capital, Lusaka. I had very little dollars left and I had to work. I needed to find a job, repair or maintenance of vehicles or any kind of job.

In Zambia, I needed to have a work permit in order to apply for employment. However, I did not have the time or the money to remain there to comply with the requirements. A couple of days later, I turned away my thought towards my journey.

I went to Livingston, the historical town, and to Victoria Falls on Zambezi River. I stayed for a couple of days at the border of four countries, Zambia, Zimbabwe, Namibia, and Botswana, at a small town called Sesheke.

Since childhood, one of the things I loved to do was touring historical sites, museums, and libraries to get information and to discover about the ancient history of Africa and the people. I was fortunate to reach many of such places on my way.

Since I began this leg of journey, I did not make contacts with my family or friends back in Ethiopia. I thought about them constantly and could not avoid worries.

Being alone in a foreign country in a different environment required more awareness all the time. Even when I go for a short walk, I should be alert and observant.

Before my visa expired, I had to get out of Zambia. I had a small map as a guide. I always preferred to use the shortest route. I had little money left, a couple of hundred dollars that I carried from Kenya.

On 27 April 1994, I left to Malawi, through a small Zambian border town called Chipata. Later that day I got to the capital city Lilongwe. Malawi is a less populated very peaceful small country.

One of the things I noticed throughout my journey was the similarity of the language, culture, and tradition among the African nations. The language Swahili exists almost everywhere.

I kept on asking myself why was my country different, why was that we did not have a close relationships with African countries. Emperor Haile Selassie had good connections with the West than with the African countries.

Lilongwe is the capital of Malawi, relatively small for a city with very few buildings here and there. It is easy to get to anywhere without difficulty. Food and accommodation are cheap and affordable.

I stayed in Malawi longer than I anticipated. It is a country largely covered with green natural beauty. I made quick friends as I always do, but there was something always in my mind, which I should not forget.

I am not a tourist. I had a mission and could not manage to stay longer than I could afford. I decided to get out of Malawi within the next two days, but there was something that held me back.

The next morning when I walked down town, I met three Somalians. They told me, 'You need to go to the UNHCR office for registration.' But I did not clearly understand what they meant.

Shortly I went to the UNHCR building to find out what was going on, and when I got there, I met so many refugees who came from different parts of African countries, among them were, Ethiopians.

Solomon, Samson, and Chuchu were among some of the Ethiopian nationals who had been registered as asylum seekers at Malawi. The UNHCR provides assistance for all refugees, irrespective of their nationality.

I become closer to some of the Ethiopians who had already been there and were waiting for the appropriate time to travel to South Africa. None of them had a legal travel document.

Four of us lived together—myself, Samson, Solomon, and Chuchu. Each of us have different and disturbing history. A few of them had been arrested and tortured and escaped from detention. It's all about political activities back in Ethiopia.

Commonly all of us have been affected in many different ways through the political storm in our country. They do not need to know about my story. I did not want to open up. It was not my time.

Whenever I met someone, we started talking about the past, and I listened to what he or she went through. It could be politics or something else, but I always kept mine sealed.

Two months later in mid of June 1994, four of us decided to cross over to Mozambique through a small village called Muanza. Shortly after crossing the border, we had been detected by the immigration officers at the border post and taken to their office for questioning.

After a short investigation, all of us were released and allowed to cross the border freely. And after three days of difficult journey, in the first week of July 1994, we landed at the east coast port city of Beira, in Mozambique.

The following day we reported to the UNHCR office for assistance. They provided us with temporary accommodation, at a small town called Dondo. Then we did not have money to sustain ourselves even for a short time, and we needed their support badly.

The Dondo camp is about 12 miles away from Beira. We met with two guys, who came from West Africa, from Ghana and Liberia, who have been at the camp for the last two weeks, Michael and Thomas.

The two young men travelled thousands of miles to seek for a better life, without any travel documents; it's about four months since they had come out of their home town. They had been through many kinds of problems.

We did not get much of the assistance we needed. The authorities were not keen to solve any of our problems. For two weeks we remained ignored in the dirty small shelter.

The Dondo shelter reminded me of the small huts at Fashim detention center. None of my new friends knew about my previous experience, here we were free to go, and not under captivity. We have decided to keep on moving, to vacate the Dondo camp.

There is a long journey ahead of us before we reached the South African border. We began our journey from Beira to Maputo in a small bus. After three days of difficult journey, we reached the city of Maputo.

One of our concerns was the immigration requirements, security checkups, and roadblocks. The three guys did not have travel documents. Fortunately, we arrived at Maputo without problem.

Michael and Tomas chose to stay behind at Dondo. They had a plan to go to Europe or anywhere else out of Africa, hiding in the cargo ship, *Stow Away*, from the sea port of Beira, located in the city.

Maputo is one of the old and dirty impoverished Portuguese colonial cities; even though Mozambique was an independent state, the colonial footprints still existed and was visible everywhere in the city. The giant monuments were the reminder of colonial masters.

The Portuguese language is the main and widely spoken among the Mozambique nation. English or other language users would definitely find it difficult to communicate. Sometimes we use sign language as a form of communication.

Solomon, Samson, and Chuchu came up with the new idea—they wanted to remain in the capital Maputo for a while. But I disagreed with their opinion, and I left Maputo alone on 17 July 1994 to one of the smallest countries in Africa known as Swaziland.

Swaziland is a small country lying between South Africa and Mozambique. Before midday, I landed in Mbabane, the capital of Swaziland. I did not have enough money, so I decided to sell my camera, and I went to the second-hand shops where they buy and sell goods.

As I was walking between the shops and entered one of the smaller shops, I met an Ethiopian guy by the name of Siraj, a shopkeeper who came to the city over two years ago. Siraj lived in the outskirts of the city alone in a double bedroom flat.

We communicate in our language. He bought my camera in addition; he offered me one of his rooms. I stayed with Siraj for the duration of three days, and we became friends.

Relatively I had a good time, and it was my first time in a home environment. His intention was to go to South Africa, however; he changed his plan when he found a job in Mbabane. I was getting closer to the biggest city in Africa, Johannesburg.

Fortunately, wherever I go, I meet new people who would understand my condition. I spend time for a while, share information, and move on again, to the next destination. That was how it went since I started my journey.

I remember all the people I met since Hoha, at the border town of Kenya. I had a collection of good and bad memories. few of the people I met have already passed away before they accomplish their journey, some of us find ourway to South Africa.

The morning of 19 July 1994 would be my last leg of the journey. I boarded a bus from Mbabane, and after a short travel, I get to the border town, which lay between Swaziland and South Africa. I cross over to the border of South Africa without difficulty, and I board a minibus on the main road to Johannesburg.

Johannesburg is a big city, very crowded and bizarre. Everything is moving fast, and distinctive from the rest of Africa in many ways. They called it 'the golden city'. Johannesburg is the economic capital of Africa.

I slipped away through the crowed to find a small hotel or a room where I could rest and collect myself; fortunately, I found a small room not far from the bus station.

During my stay, I observed Johannesburg. The city never sleeps. I began to wonder how I could possibly adjust myself with the situation there in South Africa.

At the time, South Africa was in transition. It was a time of freedom. A time of change from one-party apartheid state to a democratically elected majority rule. A new era, new politics, so much excitement.

The next morning I went to a coffee shop nearby, and I met a guy, a refugee from Sudan. His name was Osman. He spoke Arabic. He recognised me, that I came from far, the Horn of Africa. He knew I was an Ethiopian.

After a short conversation, he wanted to know if I would be interested to join him for a cheaper accommodation. I accepted his offer, since I did not have enough money. I chose to stay with him and see how it went.

He guided me to one of the apartments commonly called the Hillbrow area.
He introduced me to a South African woman, Mrs Dorel Cole, who lived with her family in a small flat. Later I found out Hillbrow was the most violent and deadliest area in Johannesburg.

Mrs Cole was a pensioner who lived with her disabled husband, children, and two grandchildren. As a stranger, when I stepped into her house, she made me feel welcome and that was a good sign.

Mrs Cole and her family were truly generous and kind-hearted. I was very touched by the warm reception I was given during my week-long stay at their flat. I promised to myself to be in contact wherever I might be.

South Africans seem to be more suspicious. Whenever approached by a stranger, they prefer to ignore or they would want to know who the person was before they respond.

Once they identified who the person was, they are very welcoming and very helpful. In a short space of time, they are able to understand and study the character, attitude, and tendency of individuals.

For any questions asked, they would give short and direct answers always in a hurry. They did not have the time or the patience for long explanation, unlike other people I met in Africa.

I was not comfortable in Johannesburg, and I did not get to see any of my friends who left behind in Maputo, Mozambique. I decided to carry on my journey to Cape Town as the final destination.

On Wednesday, 22 July 1994, I boarded the blue train from Johannesburg to Cape Town. It was a long journey. The next day, the 23 July '94, after midday, I arrived at the Cape Town station.

Through my long journey, I have learned how to react and approach new people and the environment. Whenever and wherever I get to a new town or city, the first thing I would do was to get safe and low-cost accommodation.

I walked out of the Cape Town train station. As I walked through the central city to find a place, incidentally I met a gentleman, and I asked him what I was looking for, accommodation. Instead, he asked me many unrelated questions.

He then thought for a while and said to me that if I was willing to go with him, he would offer me free accommodation, and in return, I had to look after his property. The deal was very short and simple.

I thought to myself. I have nothing to lose, but I needed to see the place before I accepted the offer, and he drove me off to Grassy Park, at the out skirt of Cape Town to his property. I thought for a while and decided to stay for a short period of time as long as it cost me nothing.

It was a small house standing alone, but there were houses scattered in a distance. It was a farm area. A single-room house with no electric light or hot water. For me it was not a big deal; I was used to such environment.

Before he left, he briefed me about the area with some instructions I need to adhere to—no alcohol, drugs etc.—which I had never been associated with anyway. He was a religious man, over sixty, Mr Basher.

One week later, I went to the Home Affairs and submitted the application form as an asylum seeker. After a short interview, I was given temporary work permit, which had to be renewed every six months.

Once or twice a week, I visited the city center, hoping to find my friends. It was a rainy season, very cold and uncomfortable to walk around. I was not used to this kind of weather, but I had to learn and adopt the harsh weather.

The days are shorter in winter and longer in summer, quite a different climate from the equatorial region of Africa. I had to associate and adopt myself with the new environment. The change of weather could not affect me. I had to see the long term, the future.

One afternoon in August, I went to Cape Town, a place where most asylum seekers gathered. Incidentally, I met one of my friends standing among many refugees—Solomon, who refused to go to Swaziland with me, who was left behind in Mozambique, Maputo.

He arrived at Cape Town two days ago; he had very little money left. He was desperately looking for a place to stay and needed my assistance as he had no where to go.

I was happy to be with someone I knew. We went together to Grassy Park where I stayed. On our arrival, I called Mr Basher, the owner of the house, to seek permission for Solomon to stay in the house. Mr Basher accepted my request and Solomon became the new member in the house.

As time progressed, Solomon and I became very close friends; occasionally, we went to the city center. Sometimes we met two or more Ethiopians, new arrivals who were confused, stressed, with no money or place to go. We took them to Grassy Park, to our place.

Two months later, our number increased to more than eight; some of the names were Samson, Asres, Tigist, and Chuchu. After a couple of weeks' stay, a few of them moved out and started doing small businesses, selling variety of goods on street corners of Cape Town.

We support each other as one big family, who ever get anything useful, we always share among ourselves, but there are people who do not like immigrant. One Saturday midnight, towards the end of September 1994, something unexpected happened.

There was someone from the neighborhood, who did not like our presence in the area and decided to do something about it, to get rid of all of us collectively, we were unaware and there was no any indication or suspicious in our part.

Late in the evening, someone broke in to our house carrying a plastic container of acid, we were asleep and completely unaware, and he sprinkled all over the house emptying the Jar and went out of the house unnoticed.

Suddenly I smell something irritating and when I wake me up, immediately I recognised the smell. It was a Sulfuric acid solution, commonly used as electrolyte for the use of car batteries. The small house was saturated with the fumes of the acid.

Immediately I shouted and nervously all of us ran outside to save our lives. Shortly we noticed a black man standing outside carrying the plastic jar. He was drunk and could not speak properly.

When we observed closely, we knew the man. He was very friendly, but now he had changed, spoke his intentions with many kinds of threats. Initially he wanted to burn the house and destroy all of us together.

His name was Mansur. Originally a black Christian person, he converted and became a Muslim later. Mansur claimed he was a coloured man and did not want to be called as a black person. I do not know why he switched his race.

We all stood outside confused and for a while did not know what to do. We did not establish relationships with the community. We were always respectful and keep our distance. Certainly, we were not a threat to anyone.

Shortly three of us went to the nearest petrol station and made a call to the police station. An hour later, two white police officers arrived with their police van.

We explained everything to the police officers, and they questioned the culprit as he stood outside. He did not deny and told them the truth, his intention was to destroy all of us and trying to justify as if he has done the right thing. He said, 'These are illegal immigrants. We do not need them in our community.'

The two police officers shied away from the objective of our case. They declined to investigate the matter. Instead they turned on us, and they did it aggressively and disrespectfully with intimidatory remarks. I personally appreciated the culprit for his honesty to speak out his intention.

I believe generally racism is a stigma created in human mind. The black man may have felt threatened by our presence, but I think the sense of humanity should always come first. It can affect anyone and there should not be an excuse for racism.

We all have legal document, which indicates as an asylum seekers, issued by the South African Government. The police officers searched through our belongings and asked us many intimidating questions, but we were not in a possession of any illegal items. Shortly they left without a word as nothing has happened as we stood outside in the cold.

It was a disappointment to find ourselves treated inhumanely by the criminal more over, by the action of the two police officers, basically who are regarded as law enforcement agents.

As we all know language is a powerful tool of communications. And more likely it could give an advantage to the offender who speaks the language than to the victim who does not.

Mansur was talking to the police officers in their own language; it is likely that that was what happened in our case. We assumed xenophobia was the main factor; we decided to vacate the area without delay.

The next morning I informed the owner of the house, Mr Basher, about the incident. Mr Basher knew the person but declined to take any action. Instead, he advised us to leave with immediate effect.

Two days after the incident, we scattered into different parts of Cape Town's suburbs. In a big city, accommodation is very expensive, and most of all, the owners require a South African ID document to rent a house. We had to go separate ways. However, occasionally, we saw each other and never lost contacts.

Approximately a week later, I found a job, at the workshop, at a petrol station in Athlone area, a place called Gatesville in Cape Town, I did not have a specific job, I do car wash, mechanical repair, welder, petrol attendant, tire repair . . .

Whatever comes in that workshop, I had to be part of it. I had to assist in everything. It was not my choice, but due to the circumstances, I have to do it to overcome my personal problems. I have also learned other techniques in the process.

Mr Adams, the owner of the garage, is wealthy and young looking for his age. He has interviewed me about the job two days prior to the employment. I think he was satisfied with my performance and wanted more of my service. He needed to know where I was staying.

He asked me if I am interested. He would provide me a room to stay for free. I accepted the offer without hesitation, because accommodation was my biggest problem. He took me to his house and guided me to the tiny room attached to the main house at the back. He said, 'This is your room.'

One of the workers hinted to me, 'Mr Adams is the greediest person on the planet.' I knew he needs something in return. Whenever a free offer is given in some cases, there would be a kind of string attached to it, a free service in return or something else, and I am aware of his move.

I was instructed to 'clean the yard and feed the dog every morning'. That was exactly what he told me the next morning just before we leave his house. I was not happy with the additional job I was given. I am paid every week very little. He knew my problems and I had no option.

Three months later, I was able to save small amount of money, which could take me further out of exploitation. I needed to stand up for myself. I gained momentum and felt confident. I said to myself I would get a better job, and I decided to move out of exploitation.

It was at the beginning of December 1994. While I was thinking of my options, one of my friends Solomon suddenly appeared. He came to the garage looking for me. It was a surprise visit.

I told him the workload and my unhappiness. He then made an arrangement to stay with him in Woodstock area. Finally I informed Mr. Adams and his family, 'I am done. I am leaving.'

He was willing to offer more money, but I was disappointed in him, and his money could not change my mind. I have seen him in many occasions that he has no morality. I was very firm on my decision; the wife and the two teenaged girls did not want me to leave.

Besides the job I did, I was part of the family. They trusted me. Whenever they went for a holiday or on any other occasion, I was the one who looked after the house and the girls.

When I left that Saturday morning, I left without my bag. His wife refused to give me my bag. She thought I might change my mind. I appreciated her concern. She knew exactly why I was leaving. I was treated unfairly. I thanked her for her understanding and kindness. I promised I would be in touch wherever I might be.

Moira Henderson is a two-storey building that belonged to the city council, which is located in Woodstock where Solomon and many people live, old house with many rooms, and it serves as an accommodation for low-income people, for those who earn little or have no jobs.

Solomon introduced me to the manager, Mr. Peter, and I paid the required amount of fee one month in advance, and I was given a room with six people to share that included Solomon. At the time in total there were about forty people living at Moira Henderson House, belonging to different races.

Solomon was working as a driver for a private company. We supported each other and the rest of my friends working in different locations and most of them were self-employed, selling different kinds of goods such as cigarettes, sweets, chocolates, chips, etc. on the street corners.

I settled at Moira and a couple of days later, I started looking for a new job, but in between, something unexpected happened just after one-week at Moira Henderson House.

Saturday, 18 December 1994, at midday, I was sitting in Small Park, in Woodstock, very close to where I lived. It was a quite and sunny day. I was alone by myself, relaxing in the hot sun.

I was about to leave when nine young men approached me from behind as I was sitting. When I turned and looked back, they pretended as if they were passing through, but suddenly, they stopped. Some of them had short and long sticks in their hand.

I was surrounded before I noticed and as I was sitting, one of them requested a cigarette and before I respond they started beating me with a stick from behind, boxing kicking all over my body so fast and so hard.

I was confused and terrified, did not even have time to think what was going on. Approximately five minutes later everything was over. I was terrified, shocked, very nervous, and disturbed. I never expected such attacks in a broad daylight.

I could see many people standing as a spectator in a short distance, but were not prepared to be involved. I found it difficult to understand why they stood silently as observers while I was attacked by the gagsters.

I was very angry and too weak to get up and vacate the area immediately. I felt the cuts on my face, bleeding and scratches on my chest. I was top naked; they tore and took my jacket along with my shirt.

My passport and all the money I saved, including those few dollars that I carried for a long time had gone. Moreover my head started shaking non-stop and uncontrollably. I had to stay where I was on the ground for a while to clear my mind to calm down.

I needed to get up and go, before the pain went through my body. Henderson House was not far from the park. I was angry, frustrated, and ashamed. I had severe headache. Soon, I started walking slowly.

When I got closer, I could see Solomon standing outside Henderson House next to the main gate. At first, he did not recognise me. By then my face was swollen and covered with blood, and my hands were still shaking.

I could not stand the growing of pain in my ribs, and the next day I went to one of the hospitals. After the X-ray and examination, the doctor informed me my ribs were fine and no cracks had occurred. He put me on medication to ease the pain.

I had to calm down in order to put myself back on track. Most of my friends came for a visit and shared with me their views about the gangsters and how they operated and attacked.

Especially African immigrants are easy prey, in the townships and big cities many of them have been killed brutally. The government could not stop the killing nor admit it. Refugees can be identified in many ways, by their accent and unable to speak the local language properly.

Three days later, I went to the police station and reported the matter. The police provided me with an affidavit confirming that my personal belongings had been stolen, and that was it. There was no further investigation. The police also did not give much attention if the victim happened to be an immigrant and a black person.

Soon I started to look for a job. Solomon and some of my friends were willing to assist me with whatever I needed, and I was very grateful for that, but I wanted to overcome the challenge by myself as I always did.

On 19 January 1995, I was employed at the sea port as a tally clerk for a company that exported fruit to many different countries around the world. I was given two weeks of training, and I was back on track again.

The gangsters seemed to be living in the same area where I lived, but I could not identify them by their looks. After they attacked me, they walked away gently. They did not even bother to escape.

At the time the gagsters knew no one would arrest them, they were confident they would think they are powerful and untouchable. I am able to recognise the face of the youngest of the group, nine or ten years old boy. He kicked me on my face, repeatedly.

Now over ten years later and when I thought about him, I might not be able to recognise his face, but I completely forgave him. He would be an adult and must be regretting what he had done.

Henderson house is more than average night shelter, the residents gather at the TV room after work or during weekends. When I was not working that was the place where I like to spend my time, watching different programs, on the TV screen.

As time progressed, I became closer to some of the people who resided at the Henderson House. One of them was a young woman by the name of Andrea Liebenberg.

She asked me, 'What is wrong with your face?' after she discovered the scratch marks on my face from the incident took place at the park and 'why is your head shaking
My problem was when I met people, they usually noticed and asked why my head was shaking. I do not tell them why, but I felt embarrassed every time they mentioned about my head. I could not avoid the shaking of my head; it started unexpectedly and got beyond my control.

I told Andrea about the gang incident at the park. She advised me what was likely to happen when confronted by the group of gangsters—n many cases knife stabbing or bullet wounds and in some cases even death.

It was the beginning of our relationship., As time went by, we became closer. She was caring and very honest—Andrea Liebenberg, a third-year student at Cape Town College of Education.

Capetonians are cautious and alert in every move they make. They do not trust and usually avoid talking to strangers for a variety of reasons. I had to learn and live the way they did, but I found it very difficult to adjust myself with the situation so quickly; it will take time.

Most of my friends were very busy doing business. Often we do not see each other for weeks and some of them moved away to different parts of South Africa, to Durban and Pretoria.

My nervous problem getting better, since I started attending at the hospital the medicines, the counseling from the Doctor was very helpful, every three months I attend the hospital for observation.

The pain in my shoulder and ribs slowly disappeared. Thanks to Andrea she used to rub me every night whenever I came from the job, and everything looked better and better as the days progressed.

Sometimes when I sit alone, I start to think and wonder about the past and what lies ahead in the future. I was confronted with many challenges in different times. Many kinds of incidents, in danger and in happiness; it was my time to change. I wanted to share my life with someone. I wanted someone in my life.

At the beginning, Andrea and myself became just friends. There was really no love between us, but we cared and had a good friendship. However, things started to change as we got to know each other.

Andrea was a very sick and unhappy child. Even though she did not mention the cause, she suffered lots of pain on her back and hips. Sometimes I popped in to her room and tried to comfort her and give her a hug, just to say I was there for her.

Sometimes she could not even walk; she had pains in every part of her body. I felt very sad, and it brought me closer to her more than ever before, and the closer I became, I start to be more concerned.

Gradually I became stable and tried to adjust myself with the environment, getting to know more and more people at work and at Henderson House. I spoke quite a few languages. I am a quick learner of languages.

I hardly understand Afrikaans language, the colonial language inherited from Holland. I would assume, because of the trauma associated with the assault by the gangsters during the attack, they swearing at me in Afrikaans language at the park in Woodstock.

They were yelling, shouting, and swearing at me in Afrikaans language, but the language had done nothing wrong, and I need to learn the language in order to make life easy, especially in Cape Town.

14 February '95 was our first date. I gave her a bunch of flowers wishing her a happy Valentine's Day, and we spent the rest of the day together. That was the beginning.

It requires much more time to get to know each other, but considering my personal experience in life and my age, I thought it would be better to be with someone. I was turning thirty-four, and she was thirty.

One afternoon I asked Andrea for a walk. I collected myself and asked the question I had never asked before. I called her by name, and I asked if she had ever thought about marriage and followed the big question, 'Would you marry me?'

She stopped and looked at me for a while at first. She hesitated to answer or talk about marriage. After she gasped for air she said, 'No, I never thought about marriage and cannot marry you.'

I never expected a negative response and felt so bad. It was just a simple request, and she rejected my proposal. Clearly, she needed time to know me better. I accepted her opinion and shift my thoughts and I promised to myself, never to raise the idea again.

We remained good friends as we used to be. I did not want to spoil our relationship. Although I was disappointed with her response, I had to forget about the marriage and go on with my life.

Sometimes I ask myself, when do I get married? My life could not be on the move all the time, I need to have different life style, I need someone more than a friend, I want to experience marriage life.

I knew very little about Andrea's background and her personal character. The only similarity between us seems to be not having a close family around us and both of us were in the lower income group of the society.

Andrea was not the way she looked; the real Andrea was so different. It was about her past. It had a big impact in her life. It changed her character. That is what has made her into what she is now.

She usually diverted my questions about her childhood. I also did not want to cause her sense of discomfort. Whenever I ask about her past, she always become irritated and avoided my questions.

I understood there must have been something terribly wrong in her past, and I refrained from asking about her past. After all why would I need to know about her past? I made up my mind not to ask again for marriage.

Andrea never gave up the thought of marriage. She went to her friends to sought for advice without my knowledge. Deep down she wanted to marry me, but her friends strongly opposed to my proposal.

I was completely a stranger to everyone around, and on top of that, I am a foreigner from a different race and culture. She was the only one who knew very little about me. To be honest if I would be in their position, most probably I would react the same way.

One has to go a long way to prove oneself of trustworthiness, personality, or good character and to carry out responsibilities; these are some of the measurements commonly required by the society.

I have nothing to prove. I did not have the patience or the time or the will to go about in this route. I also had to think about other things important to me—getting a better job, my life, my families, my colleagues, and so on so forth.

A week later, she decided by herself and made up her mind she said, 'I accept your proposal.' From what I understood from the tone of her sound she needed to know my response very quickly and wanted a positive answer, but I declined to give my answer immediately. I said to her 'I would think about it.'

I never got to sleep all night long, thinking over and over again, because I had already set my mind for a friendship, no more, no less, on other hand, I could achieve something important.

If I get married to a South African citizen, I could get permanent resident permit in South Africa, which can lead me to acquire citizenship, but that was not my initial thought at the beginning. I had no intention to acquire resident permit or citizenship through marriage.

My decision was mainly based on the desire to settle down and form a family, but there could always be unseen risks and responsibilities, which might emerge afterwards.

I was not afraid of that. I should respond as it comes. I always believed for any problem, no matter how hard it looked, there would always be a solution, a way out.

I survived many challenges. I do not think marriage is more difficult than to live in the Fashim forest under captivity in horrible conditions, but this marriage took me a while to decide.

Andrea needed my answer very quickly. She did not have the patience and often she got frustrated, frequently sending her friends to my room, several times a day, demanding my answer.

If she had known what I went through previously in my life and how I was affected, she may not be willing to marry me, but I remained optimistic and positive.

Three days later I told her my decision. 'I am willing to be with you to be together.' I made my commitment to marry her. She was very happy. That was what she wanted to hear.

On 2 March 1995, we went together to the marriage office. The lady at the office conducted the legal process. Soon the marriage ordeal was completed and we become legally married couples.

A month later, Andrea told me, 'There would be a big surprise for you.' I did not know what it could be, and most probably it would be the wedding and nothing else.

I was nervous when I met the guests at the wedding. Everything went well. The more I went in to it, I became relaxed and more confident. It was a happy conclusion. Solomon was my best man.

After the wedding long gone, and as we led a normal life, something started to emerge. It was about Andrea's attitude and unpredictable behaviours. It was very unfortunate our relationships quickly turn around.

It was all about her past, which she kept it secret from everyone, if the truth comes out she might be afraid of rejection, however the truth will be revealed when the time comes.

I could sense something terribly wrong in her past. She became violent, lots of anger, breaking furniture, yelling at me night after night; she became out of control.

When she gets angry, she become powerful and very hard to calm her down, it was my first experience to witness such character and human emotions.

I could not possibly explain how she displayed her anger. It was outrageous and very frightening. Although I tried to keep myself cool, the circumstance did not allow me to remain silent.

It was just a couple of months since we got married, and she had deep buried anger. I strongly suspect it had something to do with men, but I am unable to explain, to be honest I was afraid to ask her, at the beginning I was confused and did not really know what to do.

If I made the slightest attempt to get her to calm down by talking with kind words, she became more agitated and aggressive, throwing me to one side with enormous power. Her face and her looks in general became more of a devil character.

It was just few months in to our marriage, and I did not have the capacity or the ability to handle such matters. Constantly, she abused me verbally as well as physically.

She scratched me, she pushed me, she beat me, she threw me, she tried very hard in every possible way to draw me in to the violence, but I never tried to push her or hurt her in any way verbally or physically.

Through many experiences, I began to sense something very odd. I may not be the one she is taking to. She perhaps replaced me with someone in her thoughts, in her imagination.

I was very patient, to be honest. Sometimes I was scared of her, and for days, we did not communicate, and what hurt me the most was she was always in denial and never admitted of wrongdoings afterwards.

Sometimes she drove me crazy, pushed me to the limit, and when I got to the critical point, my head started shaking uncontrollably in a way that was obvious to every one, and that made it worse.

When Andrea noticed the problem I had, she began to feel a sense of guilt and stopped abusing and upsetting me, but that did not last long. Within a short span of time she started all over again.

Sometimes I used to pretend as if I am sick, just to make her believe that she should leave me alone and to get off from the hook for a while, but when I think now, what I did then was very stupid.

She is very demanding and manipulative. She needed to hear every single day how much I loved her, and there was nothing wrong with that, but it seemed to be not working.

Gradually, I began to understand her character. She liked to control and overpower men of any kind, but she approached women cautiously. I think she was afraid of them.

I was very careful not to be judgmental. I have tried everything to control the situation. Moreover, when she got out of hand, it become very hard to bring her back to normal. Intimidations, blackmailing, and swearing were her weapons to drive away any kind of objections to her demand.

Andrea is a bubbly, cheerful, and lovable innocent girl when she was seen from outside however, she is a very difficult and obscure person at home. I would say she has a split personality.

She has a tendency of acquiring everything by threatening or often by using force. She has no consideration of our financial ability. Whenever she gets depressed, she goes on a shopping spree on credit. I think I knew Andrea more than she knew herself.

Sometimes I became upset and irritated of her friends, who do not want to stand up and tell her what she was doing was wrong, but most of them did not know, as she pretended and kept them away from her private activity.

I need to know the root cause of her anger, because I had done nothing wrong. I always loved her and comforted her, but her attitude towards me was depressing and affecting me constantly.

In many instances, she had told me, I am not the cause of her anger. I think that was just to keep me down and she was good at that, but why would she take it out on me, and why would I feel responsible for the guilt of others.

For a long time, I was clueless about what to do, but finally I made my decision—separation would be the best solution for both of us. I was forced to leave her alone and move on with my life, due to the circumstances. I had no other option.

Towards the end of June 1995, late one afternoon, I came home from the job. As usual she was upset about something I did not know. I could not even ask her politely. I learned my lessons in a very hard way. I did not want to hear aggressive or abusive responses.

The problem was if I kept silent, she started nagging, or I would be blamed for not giving her enough attention or something else. I felt that, as if I was caught between something I could not explain.

That evening, she screamed through the night. We never went to sleep. Early in the morning I went outside. I could see her standing by the window, in the upper floor in the room where we lived.

I called her and I said, 'I am not coming tonight. I would be staying with my colleagues.' I had already decided the previous night, but I was afraid to talk to her face-to-face, as she was unpredictable.

Before I finished my last word, she said, 'If you have decided to leave me now, I am going to jump and kill myself from where I am.' She was moving towards the edge of the big window as she spoke.

I was very shocked and terrified. I said to her, 'I will come back. Please do not do it.' I begged her not to jump and kill herself. I went to my job, occupied with bad thoughts, and my mind did not function properly. When I came back in the evening, she sounded better, but heavily depressed.

I could not explain why, but I changed my mind, and I stayed with her, but I always thought of other options. The love between us was shadowed by fear. I think I began to feel sorry for her than love her. That is not a good indication; there should be love between married couples. Our love had eroded and faded away due to bad relationship.

Solomon had moved to Durban City, and there was nobody to seek advice. And I do not have any knowledge about human psychology. We need to speak to someone; there may be help available.

Andrea did not want to say a ward about what was going on in her mind. She kept all her past secrets to herself. I told her she needed help, and we needed to see someone. She agreed with my idea.

The first time we went to a woman whom she knew very closely. Although Mrs Pricilla was not a professional psychiatrist, she gave us an idea of how we could improve our relationship and reconcile with ourselves.

Two weeks later in February '96, we went to see a professional psychologist. He was prepared to help us, but she was not willing to open up her baggage. I think she did not want him or anyone else to know about her past.

Soon afterwards, Andrea realised she had to tell to someone, and she decided to tell me everything from the beginning, most all what was affecting her for so many years—but not all at once. I think she needed to observe my reaction in every stage before she drained everything. I promised I would never be judgmental.

*   *   *

Andrea was born on 15 October 1965 in the small town of Western Cape, in Paarl. Her father was George Farmer and mother Nolin Liebenberg. Nolin was a close relative of George Farmer.

Nolin, as a young girl of fourteen, came from the north-western region, from Namaqualand, to stay with her uncle, who was a married man with nine children, George Farmer.

At the age of sixteen, Nolin was sexually abused by her own relative, Uncle George, and soon she became pregnant. That was the turning point and the beginning of her unrest and misery in life.

At the end of her pregnancy and as a young girl, the inexperienced Nolin had to deliver baby Andrea all by herself.

Nolin was forced to lie about the real father of baby Andrea. She created an imaginary father, a person who never existed, who was assumed to be working at the train station.

George Farmer was among those who earned very little. Nolin had no salary or benefits, but she had been working for him for many years for nothing.

Two years later, unfortunately, Nolin had another pregnancy, and George Farmer become the father of her second child. She had to lie again about the father of the unborn baby.

George Farmer was a husband and a father who controlled and maneuvered everything under the roof of that house, except his wife. He was so fearful of his wife. Carefully he planned and created a perception among the family and neighbors that he was not the father of both babies.

During the second pregnancy, she developed complications. This time she had to go to the hospital as a matter of urgency. Subconsciously, she revealed the name of the real father, George Farmer.

A few days later, he was arrested by the police for statuary rape. However, she defended him. She gave a false statement to the police. She said, 'He was not the father of the children.' The case was dropped, and he was set free. Nolin did not get credit for that. Instead she was expelled from the house with two kids.

Gradually the innocent Nolin transformed into a violent, angry, aggressive, and often-depressed woman. She did not choose to be like that, but she had been crafted to become that through many years of social depravation. Nolin did not trust anyone. She hated everyone including herself.

Nolin did not want to tell her past to anyone. Andrea knew very little the story about her mother's childhood life, before age fourteen, while she stayed at Namaqualaland. Andrea had no clue about her grandfather or grandmother or her extended family, except one uncle who distanced himself from Nolin many years ago.

Andrea did not want to drain everything at once, and also I was not prepared to listen to everything that her mother went through, but it could be an indication of what Andrea's future would likely be.

Little Andrea was two years old when John was born. Nolin had to leave the house with her two children. She stayed with her aunty somewhere not far from George Farmer's house in Paarl. For many years, Andrea did not know whether the aunty was a true blood relative or just anyone whom they call aunty.

Couple of years later she had two more babies, a year apart, from different fathers. The elder one was Timothy, who died before his first birthday, and the younger one was Christie.

Her aunty was an alcoholic and known for her abusive character. Nolin could not manage to stay longer. She was forced to move out with Andrea and John, leaving Christie behind by her aunty.

The aunty gave Christie away to another man, a stranger. Few years later, the unknown man moved away with the child without notification to an unknown location.

Before long the aunty died, and there was no trace of Christie, and that was the end of the little boy. Christie was not adopted through a legal process in a proper manner. He was just given away.

Nolin lived in a Cape Town area called Bellville with two kids, on and off the streets. At the end, she found a boyfriend by the name of Charles who was working at a bakery.

He earned very little every week. The owner of the bakery provided him a place to stay for the night, a parking garage. And that was what Nolin was looking for, a place to stay for a while.

Charles was a good-looking middle-aged man. Not only was he an alcoholic, he was also a drug addict and an extremely violent person. He was arrested several times for various criminal activities.

When Charles came to their life, Andrea was eight and her brother John was just six years old. They both are young to question their mother when the stranger presents himself as a stepfather.

As time went by, whenever Charles got drunk, he beat the children violently. Especially, little John was the main target. He usually hung him upside down and beat him badly.

Gradually, Nolin realised Charles was unpredictable and a very dangerous man. He could never be trusted. His employer was never concerned about what he was doing outside of his job as long as he got cheap labor.

Nolin loved her children unconditionally. She defended them furiously. They were her life. They were the only assets she had, but during the day, she had to go and find a job for their food, leaving them behind.

When she was away, the forty-five-year-old Charles started to make a move towards little Andrea with evil though in his mind. He gave her sweets to bring her closer to him. Innocently little Andrea accepted his offer without knowing his intentions.

Eventually, he abused her sexually, and after that incident, she became frightened to tell her mother or anyone. She kept this big secret to herself for over thirty years. Probably, I am the first one to listen to the whole story from her mouth.

At the time of the incident, Nolin knew something had gone wrong with Andrea but did not question. That was the beginning of Andrea's miserable life. Nolin was so unfortunate, the problem carried on to her offspring, to the next generation.

A year later, unfortunately, Nolin became pregnant and gave birth to a baby boy Fernando, the only son of Charles. By then she had three kids to care for, alone and without support.

Charles could not manage to keep up with city life and decided to go out of town along with Nolin and the three kids to the farm area called Stanford, where he had been employed as a farm laborer many years ago.

Shortly after their arrival, Charles was arrested for planting dagga (hashish) in the garden. After his arrest, the property owner demanded Nolin to vacate his property immediately. Later, Nolin and her kids were placed in foster care at the Preston's family, and a year later, Charles died of natural illness inside a prison.

Initially, I had one thing in mind—to find out the root cause of Andrea's behavior, which affected our relationships tremendously. However, the story took me many years back to the deep secret of the family.

Andrea had told me part of the story, which related to her mother, of what she remembered from her childhood. I was listening and writing. In the meantime, I was able to understand and discover many things about Nolin and the kids.

*   *   *

Andrea was a product of rape. She was also abused by the boyfriend of her mother, Charles. She must have been deeply hurt and that would be the main reason for the anger.

As time went by and Andrea got to the age of thirteen, John, eleven, and Fernando, two, they were given to a retired army officer, Mr Preston, who lived at the coast of Western Cape, in a small town called Houston.

The sixty-year-old man was known for his kindness and was highly respected in the Houston community. He was the leader of the old apostolic church and served as a priest for many years.

When he was young, he served in the army. He was a very strong and friendly man. The community looked up on him as a man of honor, a person who deserved the respect of everyone.

However, these strong characters did not reflect what he had been doing secretly at his home—stalking and abusing young girls whom he adopted. A few community members knew what he had been doing at home to the minors, but they chose to be silent, out of fear.

The department of social service provided assistance to the elderly, disabled, and children who were vulnerable, abandoned, or orphaned in different forms. Andrea and her brothers qualified the requirements.

Andrea and her brothers were adopted by Mr. Preston through the social services department. There was a woman who was working for the department in charge of placing orphan and destitute children to different family groups.

This lady had many years of relationship with Mr. Preston. After he retired from military service, he had been employed by the department of social services as a driver.

During that time, the social worker provided him with orphaned or destitute children who had nowhere to go, so that he could extract money from the state as a foster parent.

Nolin gave her children away not knowing the danger they would be heading to, which could damage their life forever. Nolin was prevented from visiting her children at Preston's house.

At the age of thirteen, Andrea was admitted to the school in standard one, and Fernando was the youngest at two years. Andrea had to take care of him and the house duties at the Preston house.

Shortly the old man revealed himself, in the first instance she become terrified screamed and stopped him. That was the beginning. He warned her that if she ever told to anyone or ran away to the neighbors or police, she would face severe punishment.' She still remembered those scary words.

She described him as a cruel person who had no mercy. She said, 'He abused me for many years.' She remained a sex slave. Gradually, she became angry, scared, and a disturbed child.

Andrea did not want to mention his name. A man of two faces, he was kind, gentle, and respectful during the day; at dark he became a completely different person.

From time to time, Andrea started to unravel her baggage, week after week, and month after month. During this period, she shed many tears. Gradually, I began to feel the impact in my own way.

Andrea and her brothers were treated badly and assaulted for many years by the old man. And he had a son, a traffic cop, who was over thirty years old at the time, and who shared the one-bedroom house with the Preston family.

He was a traffic cop well known in the community for his bad behavior. Not only was he an alcoholic, he was also a drug addict and very violent and abusive. His wife remained crippled mentally as well as physically, over many years of abusive relationships.

Nolin had a feeling that her children could be in danger. She had decided to do something. She went to Preston's house, breaking the rules, which prevented her from visiting. However, she was not welcomed and was dragged out of the house forcefully, and she never showed up again.

*   *   *

Two years later, at the age of thirteen, John had enough of the abuse and decided to escape. One morning he disappeared from the scene without a trace.

Andrea remained with little Fernando, angry and frustrated, having grown up with hate and fear. She suppressed her emotions and followed her education. She knew that was the only way out.

Over the years, the son of Mr. Preston assaulted Fernando badly, at the last, he also has decided just like his brother at the age of fourteen, he went missing and later he joined his mother Nolin.

Fernando did not stay long with his mother. He joined a notorious gang, and he remained on the street selling drugs and doing crimes at an early age. Andrea remained alone, faced with another abusive person, the traffic cop, the eldest son of Mr Preston.

At the age of twenty-three, Andrea desperately wanted to move out from the house of Mr Preston, but she did not know how. She made her first move. She went to the neighbors for assistance.

A few of them declined to accept her because of fear of her custodian. However, there was one family group, who was prepared to take the risk of accepting her. She remained with the family until the end of the metric exam. She still has good relationships with this particular family.

Andrea was not the only child who was abused. There were other child victims of the old man. She still remembers some of the kids who were brought by the lady from the social services.

After eight years of disappearance, one afternoon suddenly John showed up from nowhere. He was driving a stolen pick-up truck. He came to see his sister Andrea.

John, as a young boy and after he escaped from Mr. Preston`s house, he joined the Street gang group. He learned doing different kinds of crimes. He became fearless and confident and loved his sister Andrea.

He turned out to be very difficult and restless and aggressive, and shortly the former custodians who were aware of his presence in the area called the police, and he was arrested.

*   *   *

Andrea started to open and drain the toxic of the past, unfolding bit by bit during a period of several months. Initially, my main intention was to find out the motives behind her character.

One thing led to another, and I went deeper and deeper listening to the tragic story of my own wife and her family. Andrea was born with deformed hips and a disease called scoliosis, 'twisted spine', she inherited genetically from her parents.

Her father and most of her half-brothers and sisters had the same problem. Some of them have gone for hip replacement; she had a severe pain in all her joints since the age of eight.

She used to hide and pretend trying to walk as a normal person, but soon I found out her physical state. However, I was more attracted by her kindness and honesty.

*   *   *

As I mentioned previously, Andrea's desperate intention to move out of the small town of Houston eventually paid off. She had information about one specific organisation that would take care of the disabled people called the Cripple Care.

In 1989, she made it to Cape Town through the assistance of the Red Cross, and she reported to the office of Cripple Care. Finally, she was admitted as a disabled person.

At Cripple Care, she met many friends, but Andrea had one major problem. Her angry outbursts at times caused problems in communicating with people around her. She was isolated and ignored.

Fortunately, she met a woman, a social worker by the name of Kathy, different from the previous one. Kathy was running a small program at the hospital.

Kathy was an incredible woman who made a significant impact on Andrea's future. Kathy was an ordinary social worker, but she went out of her way to assist Andrea in every possible way.

Kathy found a voluntary family group, who would like to provide Andrea with accommodation and other necessities. Kathy also assisted her to claim a disability grant. That was the basic and fundamental component, as she had no income.

With favorable conditions, Andrea's state of health improved. She gained more confidence. She started focusing on her education to study further. And she applied for subsidies. Later she joined Cape Town College of Education in Mowbray.

Later that year, Andrea moved out from the family she was accommodated in and started to lead her life freely and independently in Woodstock area, at Moira Henderson House.

Andrea was accommodated at Moira Henderson House and one month later I entered the Henderson House and that was where I met Andrea the first time, the starting point of our relationships.

When I decided to find out about Andrea's past history, I never thought of the potential it could have to affect me. I spent many sleepless nights thinking about her.

I am angry with the people who destroyed her life, starting from her biological father who abandoned her, the old man and his wife, and the traffic cop who abused her for many years.

Most of all I was angry with the lady social worker who provided young children to the abusive family. Surprisingly Andrea did not forget the name of the social worker. She lived somewhere in Caledon area.

On the other hand, it helped me to understand where Andrea's anger came from, and why she behaved differently. I made a commitment to deal with her emotions sensitively and responsibly.

*   *   *

In June 1996, Andrea became pregnant with our first son Noor. For her convenience, we decided to move out to one of her closest friend's house not far from the Henderson House.

We had financial problems. I had to work very hard, twelve hours or more, seven days a week. On 12 December '96, when I came home, I was told she went for check-up to the hospital and never returned.

When I got to the hospital, I found her at the maternity ward lying on the bed, looking nervous. That was her first pregnancy, she grips my hand nervously shaking, It was her due date.

Because of her disability, Andrea could not deliver the baby normally. She needed to have a caesarean operation done. And I was allowed to join the doctors at the theatre.

Thursday evening at about eight o'clock, baby Noor was born. The nurses took him away very quickly. Minutes later, after they cleaned him, they gave him to me.

I held him close to my chest, and that was the happiest moment of my life. It was an incredible feeling. I was so excited. Noor is the first child for both Andrea and myself.

*   *   *

In the beginning of 1998, I heard the bad news. It was about the death of my dear friend Solomon. He died of a short illness unexpectedly at the age of twenty-nine.

I was devastated, depressed, and felt alone. Solomon was the one I considered as a younger brother. Shortly after his death at the Durban hospital, the body has flown back to his birthplace in Ethiopia.

While I was in Durban, incidentally, I met someone familiar to me, but I was not sure where I had met him previously. As he shook my hand, he said just one word, 'Dondo'. It clicked in my mind—he was Michael.

Michael and Thomas from Liberia. We met them at Dondo camp while we were in Mozambique. He told me, 'Thomas has flown to Europe a couple of years ago.' But he remained in Durban doing business.

*　　*　　*

Since she was born, Andrea had severe pain. She tried so many kinds of medications, but without much success, and soon after we got married, her condition deteriorated. One morning, we went to Prince Alice Hospital, where she used to go for treatment.

As we sat side by side at the waiting room, I went through her thick medical file. I noticed the doctor who diagnosed her the first time, more than two decades ago.

He had indicated in his report that besides her disability, she had been abused physically as well as emotionally.

I shifted my focus—who abused Andrea up until the age of eight? To find out why and who, I needed to go back to my memories of Paarl, where everything began, the house of her biological father, George Farmer.

Some time ago, I went to Paarl with Andrea and our son in order to gain more information about her early childhood and the relationship she had with the half-sisters and brothers during those days.

As we went in to the house, I met the eldest sister Joanne, who was ten years older than Andrea, although they looked alike. That was the first time they saw eye to eye after thirty years of separation.

Joanne told us some of the secretes, Andrea did not want to confirm or deny which she had very little memories. Andrea always defended her mother, no matter how abusive she had been.

Joanne told us everything from the beginning. She guided us to the tiny dark and untidy room next to the kitchen where Andrea was born on a Friday night on 15 October 1965.

Joanne, even long after her father George Farmer and her mother had died, did not forgive Nolin or acknowledge her children. She remembered as a child the many bad things her mother had told her about Nolin.

Joanne had a feeling of hostility towards Nolin and all her children, but Andrea never gave up. That was why we decided to pay a visit to reconcile and restore family relationships, but our effort was fruitless.

Joanne described Nolin as extremely abusive and a criminal, as the enemy of the family, stating many kinds of accusations and allegations, including the mysterious death of baby Timothy.

Nolin was abused and in turn she abused her children. Andrea also is doing the same thing to the only son she had. I do not know how to stop the cycle, but it has to stop in some way.

I have decided to confront Nolin about the numerous painful allegations and accusations when the appropriate time arrives. And I am fully aware of the seriousness and the consequences.

It was not an easy task, and it might damage my relationship with Nolin, and Andrea will not be happy with my new idea, but I decided to go ahead to find out the truth, the underlying cause.

Due the sensitiveness of the information, direct confrontation with Nolin has a big risk; everything might fall apart and out of my control. I decided to avoid any confrontation and find a better way to discuss smoothly.

One of the challenges to talk to Nolin was her violent behavior. She did not like me from the beginning. She has deep hate for everyone, especially towards men.

She is very sensitive about her past; even her daughter Andrea is afraid to ask any questions about the past. Nolin never had a stable and normal life. She was very unfortunate she had to always be on the run from herself.

As I discovered the only time she had a peaceful life was up until the age of fourteen, before she moved into the house of George Farmer, while she was at Namaqualaland. Even now over the age of sixty, she never gets to have peace of mind.

I discuss her condition with Andrea and tell her that her mother needs psychological help. Andrea agrees with the idea, but we have never tried to tell Nolin, because of her violent response.

I was getting deeper into the family's past history without knowing where to stop; on the other hand, it would probably help Andrea and myself to deal with our own problems at home and more importantly to stop the cycle of abuse.

My son needs to know Joanne and all her eight sisters and brothers. The family dispute should not be carried to the next generation, but it is not easy to bring about all the family together. There is no quick-fix solution. I could not do it by myself.

The best way to find out about her past was to be very close to Nolin and I was very polite and respectful as always do towards her or anyone else.

For many years, she pretended that she fully accepted me, but we both knew that was not real. I knew perfectly Nolin did not like me. She never trusted me. I used to be disappointed, but since I began to discover about her past, I began to understand the problems within herself.

As long as I remained a part of the family, I needed to know the driving factor for such hatefulness among the family and the reason for pretending nothing happened for so many years.

I began to understand and I do not get upset as I used to be when I was treated badly during the first years of our marriage and the more I discovered about them, the less I get irritated.

*   *   *

It has been eight years in to our marriage and usually Nolin came over for a visit and that helped me to develop a good relationship and gave me the opportunity for asking questions, which I had kept to myself for a long time.

It was all about Andrea. Why and who abused Andrea while she was a little girl? Moreover there was one very tough and painful question about the two babies and the circumstances surrounding the death of baby Timothy.

Andrea was very little by herself. She had only faint memories about Timothy. She told me, 'I only heard the scream of the baby from the bathroom, and later, the baby was found dead in boiled water.'

'Nolin blamed her friend Muriel for the death of Timothy, but she never spoke openly.' Andrea believed there was secrecy surrounding the mysterious death of the baby.

For Nolin, these secrets were deeply buried explosives. Andrea knew some of the facts, but I did not want to push her further. She was aware of the seriousness and the consequences.

I also have limitations. I did not want to go far. I knew for a fact that Andrea loves and protects her mother at all costs, but I wanted to know more about Christie who disappeared from the picture, who was missing with the stranger.

In my view, I would imagine Nolin was seeking security for herself and the children; she was unfortunate the three men who were the biological fathers denied and abandoned her along with the children.

Since then, Nolin never got to see Christie again for over thirty years. She still carried a huge burden of guilt. She has never spoken. Obviously the reality remains at the back of her mind. Andrea sometimes wishes he might be well and alive somewhere out there.

As a little girl, Andrea kept his name Christie at the back of her mind for more than three decades. She said, 'I will always remember Christie and never give up on him.'

Cautiously, I was prepared to ask Nolin during her visit about the mysterious death of baby Timothy, about Christie's whereabouts, and who abused Andrea during her childhood.

Nolin was unpredictable, and it was impossible to imagine how she would react. I knew she could do anything to avoid any of the questions concerning her past.

Nolin does not like black people in general. Clearly that was a tendency, which was inherited from the previous regime of apartheid, but what makes me confused was she does not like the whites either.

After we had our supper, we usually sit and chat about everything. It was a peaceful and cold night, and I thought this could be a good opportunity to raise some of the important questions, which has been sealed off for many years.

It was time for me to ask. Between our conversations, I mentioned the name Christie just once. Suddenly everything went silent, and Andrea remained speechless. She did not like to hear that name mentioned in front of her mother.

I needed to break the silence with a positive thought to keep the conversation going. I suggested, it would be wonderful if we knew his whereabouts or make efforts to find that out and that there is nothing wrong with that.

He could be a teacher or a professional lawyer. We might find him. He will be somewhere. I was trying to ease the tension, but Nolin rejected my idea by saying, 'You do not have the right to dig into my past.'

She stopped me from asking further questions, it might lead to another and every thing might pilled off layer by layer causing a lot of hurt, that may be the reason she shut me down.

I do not have the method or the ability to handle such matters. It could be difficult to contain once it gets out of hand, and the solutions I predict might cause more problems.

Due to the circumstances, I decided to avoid any questions concerning the death of baby Timothy; however I insisted to get answers why and who abused Andrea.

Why did she run away when Andrea was admitted to the hospital indicating the source of the information—her medical records at the Princes Alice Hospital.

Nolin was very shocked to hear that and also realise that I knew more about her than she would have thought. I could feel her anger and nervousness, but she remained completely silent.

The next day she said something purposely, which I never expected to hear: 'I wish I see him again and explain to him everything, and I would beg him for his forgiveness.' I understood it was specifically directed to Christie. My efforts had paid off.

She might be thinking there was no way out, and she had to explain, had to say something. I felt terribly sad. However, it was very encouraging, but it was very short and final. That was the last time she spoke about Christie, and I never asked again.

*   *   *

Andrea has not fully recovered from the emotional problems of her past. Although I am not a psychologist by profession, it could be difficult to imagine for anyone who went through such a terrible journey to recover in a short span of time.

Over the years, Andrea has seen many professionals because of her emotional problems, depression, inability to control her anger, and the pain in every joint of her body.

The first time when I met Andrea, she was a third-year college student, but I hardly knew about her emotional problems. It took me nearly ten years to discover who the real Andrea Liebenberg was.

Their surname is Liebenberg. I ask Andrea, 'Where is this man?' She looked at me seriously, as she always does whenever I ask difficult questions. She said, 'I do not know this man. He never existed. My mother created the surname.'

I heard an elderly coloured man saying, 'In olden times, some of the coloured people used to change their surnames, and they do not like to talk about the reason.' It was interesting, but I did not ask why.

I have no regrets marrying Andrea. I loved her with all my heart, and the more I discovered about her, I became more attached and responsible to change her life to make her happy.

One of her quality is honesty, she is completely honest. She could not be able to keep any secrets from me except her past. Our relationship growing steadily over the years.

In the first couple of years of our marriage, Andrea did not trust me, even after she gave birth to our first son Noor. I had to prove to her in many ways that it was not easy and required a great deal of patience.

At the beginning of our marriage, I did not enjoy sex, because she was a victim of rape, she regards it as a reminder of evil thought and she did not enjoy as she would have.

Personally, I am not sex driven person, I value more of loving and caring, I am fully aware of what she has been through and the impact, which affected her negatively throughout her life. In this regard, I was prepared and fully cooperative and understanding.

*   *   *

After four years in college, Andrea completed her studies successfully and graduated, and in the beginning of 1998, she became a school teacher. That was a great achievement in her life. Gradually, Andrea started to show improvement in her personality and character.

Occasionally, as a flashback, the emotions buried inside of her comes out as bad memories and she cries for hours. And she becomes depressed and starts to look at me in strange ways.

I thought confrontation would be the best way to end the past, and we have to prepare for the big day in her life. No matter how much it takes, there should be a closure. I then decided to take her to Houston, where Mr. Preston and his son, the traffic cop, lived.

In order to gain more confidence, she had to confront her worst fears face-to-face. There was no shortcut. She had many frightening nightmares from time to time, and that was tearing me apart. She had to face the devil for the last time.

One Saturday morning, Andrea, her mother, Nolin, and our little boy, Noor, who was five years old at that time, boarded a bus to Houston about 100 miles away from Cape Town.

We walked down from the bus terminal in Houston. Andrea and her mother Nolin were overwhelmed by emotion, which they had experienced more than fifteen years ago. Andrea was crying uncontrollably.

As we came closer to the house, there was a very weak old man sitting outside on the dirty floor next to the entrance. I assumed him to be a person who was mentally retarded or was a beggar.

A very old small house stood alone on the corner of the road. It had four rooms separated by thin chipboard into two sections, and it contained very old wooden furniture scattered around.

There was an old women standing in the middle of the room. Andrea was crying very loud and she was not controlling her emotions, Nolin and the old woman who was standing also start crying.

I was standing at the corner of the room confused. I did not know what to do. It was very sad moment to witness the old women crying and displaying their hidden emotions for the event, which happened many years a go.

I found it difficult to understand, and wondered how these women mysteriously communicated and expressed their hidden emotions, after so many years of separation.

After the dust settled and everything came to rest, we all sat together. They introduced to me the old woman, Gerda, the wife of the traffic cop.

Initially I thought Gerda could be the wife of the old man considering her age and her condition. She was very weak, unable to walk properly, and spoke softly.

I listened to their conversation carefully. They talked about stories of old times, about friends and families who had passed away or moved away long time ago.

There was one question in my mind. Where is the old man? Also, who abused Ann and her brothers? I couldn't wait any longer, and suddenly, I asked the question.

The old women replied pointing her finger towards the direction of the open door with a cold expression, as if it were a piece of old rug which was thrown and forgotten outside.

She said, 'There he is. He could not walk or talk.' As we stepped inside, Andrea and her mother already recognised him, but they did not tell me, and it was my first time being in that house. Andrea was crying softly.

I stood up and walked to him and looked at him carefully. He was very old, over eighty. He looked sick, and probably that was the only place allocated for him to sit.

Although he was unable to speak, he had powerful and sharp eyes, which could pierce through the skin. I could imagine what kind of man he could have been if he had not been old and disabled.

I could feel his unhappiness at our presence, but I wanted him to hear me out. More importantly, I needed Andrea and her mother to listen to what I had to say.

I spoke to him unkindly and harshly. I was so angry of the pain he caused on Andrea, her mother and her brothers, it affects us all in one way or another.

I went back and sat next to Andrea. I felt very sad, I confirmed to Andrea, 'He will never control you again' by pressing her hand.

Gerda told us the whole story, of how he abused little girls. She admitted, during those days she was a drug addict and an alcoholic. She had no control over what was going on around her.

Although she knew exactly what he was doing to the young girls, she chose to be silent because of fear. Moreover, the status he had in the community served as a shield defending him.

At the time, she was also a victim of physical and emotional abuse by her own husband, but she felt deeply sorry and partially responsible for what happened to Andrea and her brothers.

She explained about her husband, 'He was jailed for criminal activities, after he was chucked from the police service. And since he came out of the jail, he remained an alcoholic wandering on the streets of Houston.'

The wife of the old man had passed away two years after Andrea had left Houston. Andrea remembered her as mournful, a women who was not happy, since Andrea known to her however Andrea was sad of her death.

A short while later I needed to see where the rape and abuse took place. For a while, Andrea hesitated and did not want to go to the other half section, to the dark old room where many bad things happened.

As she got up, slowly I followed and walked through the rooms behind her. It was a very old and untidy small room. I started to wonder for how many years Andrea must have shed her tears in this specific room.

As we crossed the half section, she indicated pointing her finger at a very old wooden furniture and bed she used to sleep on, and just one step away there was another bed identical to that of hers.

Andrea cried in tears of the bad memories of the past. She did not want to be there, but I insisted she should calm down and collect herself to overcome the past.

She noticed, everything was unchanged and it appears to be the same old furniture are still existing since she left the house of Mr. Preston fifteen years ago.

Gerda looks very old for the age of fifty—very thin, skinny, and soft-spoken. I could imagine the effect of many years of abusive relationships, alcohol, drug, smoking . . .

Finally, it was time for us to move. As we got up slowly, we thanked Gerda for the explanation she had given us about the past. And as we walked out of the house, I noticed she was crying standing alone.

I thought she might be thinking probably the next time she may not be alive to see us again. Shortly, we went out of he house as the old woman stood alone in the dark room and as the old man sitting outside motionless.

Houston is a small town located in the Western Cape, next to the beautiful town of Hermanus, known for its holiday destination for the rich and the famous, mostly whites.

Houston is situated a few miles away from Hermanus largely dominated by poor coloured communities. The high levels of poverty, unemployment, and crimes were the main problems. That was where Andrea grew up at Mr Preston's house.

* * *

Since our last visit to Houston, Andrea became more confident of herself, very relaxed, stable, and self-controlled. Most of all, emotionally, she has shown a great deal of improvement.

One of the main factors for her emotional improvement is the churches. Through the church, she had a chance to meet different people, some of whom were very helpful.

They become close friends. They guided her on how to lead a stable life, and after school time, she joined the Bible school. Later she became a member of that particular church group, 'His People's Church'.

She started to attend the church ceremonies regularly. She became peaceful and gentle and gradually she started to show signs of growth spiritually as well as emotionally. That was very encouraging.

First I am a Muslim, and nothing could shake my faith, but my main task was to create a suitable environment for Andrea to heal from the emotional wounds of the past.

Before we got married she has promised to be a Muslim, but her tendency was more towards the Christian faith. I was fully prepared to assist her in this regard or any alternative might be helpful.

As long as we live together, the effect of her past memories will ultimately affect our relationship in many ways. Anger, fear, and depression would be difficult to deal with whenever it bounces back.

A year later since our visit to Houston, we heard the death of the old man, Mr Preston. Although he is dead and buried the damage he caused remains in the minds of many children for many years to come.

I have no previous knowledge of dealing with a person who suffers from psychological breakdown; I never studied psychophysics or any of the related subjects.

From time to time, I learn through reading books of great writers, magazines, speeches made by intellectuals about meditation, mindfulness, and awareness.

This practice helped to deal with my own problems, which I had previously, moreover, to discover myself and improve my relation ships with people of different race or colour.

*　　*　　*

Fernando, since he joined the gang, remained on the streets doing various gang-related criminal activities. In one instance, he had serious stab wounds during the fight, which broke out between the gang rivals.

He was in a critical condition and was transferred to Tygerberg Hospital in Cape Town as an emergency case, and he survived through the doctor's effort. He had a big scar visible across his abdomen.

Andrea visited him at the hospital. That was the first time she met Fernando, since he disappeared from the devil's house of the sex predator, a couple of years before I meet Andrea.

One evening as we walk down to the city centre as we usually do, we saw Fernando coming towards our direction with a heavy bandage on his left arm.

Andrea screamed, she cried they hugged each other, she was very happy to see Him alive after many years of separation and that was my first time to see Fernando, September 1998

Couple of days before we met him, he was shot by the security guard and had wounds in his left arm. He said, 'While I was trying to break in to the shop the security guard fired at me' Fernando, is not afraid of anything, he likes to tell the truth, but all about the bad things he did.

He never bothered to lay charges against those who stabbed him nearly to death or those who shot him on his arm. The gangsters may have their own method of dealing with such problems.

While he stayed with us at the Henderson House, he never stopped stealing. He breaks into the houses, cars, and steals anything he could get hold on. As far as I know, Fernando spends most of his time in prison.

I tried to give him my personal advice as a friend, but he was stubborn and restless. He came home late at night. He was unmanageable and obscure. Finally, I decided to get rid of him despite his mother's accusation.

Nolin did not liked the way I handled Fernando. She always defended her children in spite of all the criminal activities they had been doing. She still believed they did nothing wrong and were innocent.

I confronted him and decided he should move out from our house. I threw all his belongings outside. Personally, I am against of all kinds of crime, theft or using drugs and bad behaviours, but his mother hates me for that.

At the time I was very disappointed with Andrea. She was not conserned and did not show any interest or not willing to support or reject my idea. She could not protect me from her mother's vicious attack.

I did not want to live in this condition. I have decided to divorce and move on with my life, but Andrea does not want to hear that. Andrea would do anything to keep me away from such idea.

When I see how they react, I started to question myself. Are they playing me out or are they the drama queens. Sometimes the way they act is quite different from who they really are.

I need to find peaceful way of telling her my ambition based on mutual understanding that we could not live together any longer. I told Andrea my decision in a very polite and formal way that I need a divorce.

At first, she was very shocked looked at me in a strange way and start to cry she felt guilty and responsible. She abuses our son and myself constantly over the years, she new she was wrong.

When she sobers, she starts to see her mistakes clearly, the guilt and the shame follows afterwards, but never admits she was wrong. Sometimes she could not believe what she has done few moments ago.

Andrea understood my decision of inevitable separation and accepted the reality. She allowed me to move out peacefully or do whatever I wish. I moved out and stayed alone in a single bedroom in different area.

Since I moved out, seldom I used go and see my Son Noor and I discovered, they both mother and daughter have changed dramatically in a short space of time. They talked to me in a dignified and respectful way.

They both talked to me in a different tone and avoided any controlling or dominance attitudes. It was amazing when they need to be good. They become smooth and perfect.

Soon Andrea got a teaching job in England. It was about three months since our divorce. She approached me that I should get over and forget about the past. We should put our differences aside and we should be together for the sake of our son.

I agree to move back and look after our son, but I was very doubtful of remarriage. I was very happy to be with my son, and I cannot lie to myself there was still space for Andrea deep in my heart.

After I moved in and before her departure to London, her mother insisted we have to remarry and live together, and I knew that was Andrea's desire, we have arranged to be remarried on her return.

May 2001, she left for the UK. In spite of our differences, I was supportive and happy for her. Regularly we chat through telephone. She sounds very comfortable and happy in London.

It was about three months since she left and lately I had a problem getting Andrea through the telephone. She just could not return my calls, but when she calls weeks later, I discovered something was wrong.

One evening as I came from the job the phone rung, and when I picked up, it was Andrea who was crying at the other end. She said, 'I am pregnant and I am coming home soon', it was short and no detailed explanation.

I felt as if something hit me over my head, I ask how it happened, 'there was a guy I met here in London, we spend time together, when he founds out I fall pregnant he did not want to see me again', she was crying.

Although we were not married at the time, I felt shocked with disbelieve, I understood from the tone of her voice, very depressed and panicked, I am aware when she gets to this point she is suicidal.

I kept on talking, trying to calm her down. I support her idea of coming back home. I never asked about the promises she had made prior to her departure. It was not the time to ask.

That night I went to bed depressed not knowing what I should do when she came. I knew she would freak out if I asked questions in detail, but I needed to know the hows and whys.

I remember on Wednesday night we talked through telephone about her condition, and just three days later, on Saturday morning, Andrea landed at Cape Town international airport in South Africa.

I was at the airport with my son Noor waiting for her arrival. By the time she came out of the custom, I saw her ashamed and depressed, trying to avoid eye contact with me. That day we did not talk much of anything, as one would have expected after a three-month of separation.

The next morning she said, 'I am sorry I made a big mistake. I messed our life.' I thought to myself, as long as we were not married she had the right to do anything in her life. There was no need to ask forgiveness.

Two days later on Monday morning, I went to my job as usual, and later in the day, I got a call from the nurse at the hospital, saying, 'You should come to the hospital immediately.'

When I got to the hospital, the nurse informed me what had happened to Andrea. She said, 'She had a miscarriage and is very upset about the incident.'
They had to lock her away in small room at the hospital.

The nurse directed me to the room. I could hear Andrea was crying loud. I opened the door of the tiny room and when she saw me standing by the door she start crying more loudly.

I tried to calm her down, and I knew how to do it. To be there for her, that was what she needs. She was heavily depressed. She lost her job, and now the baby, and she breaks her promise, many thoughts.

The complex problems made her hopeless. I have to act as a good friend in order to bring her back to her consciousness. All she needed to know was my confirmation that I would be there for her.

As the days passed, she regained her confidence, but did not want to discuss openly why and how it happened. She preferred to seal it away as she used to do.

I remained with her and never moved out, but she and her mother insisted we should get remarried. I did not want to be locked up and give away my freedom. I had to think very hard before I made a decision.

Both mother and daughter had changed dramatically. I was convinced for the sake of our son, and finally, at the beginning of 2003 we remarried in a small ceremony at our home.

Shortly after, we remarried I wanted to discover New Zealand, hoping there could be a better chance of finding a job, may be cheaper living conditions and on long term to move my family to this part of the world.

However, work permit is one of the requirements to access for any job opportunities in New Zealand which I did not have at the time and to acquire the permit is complicated and would take much longer time than initially I thought.

There were many people who were denied, among them a South African white young man by the name of Frank, who was extremely distressed. By the time I met him he was very angry and depressed,

I comforted him just to calm him down. Later through talking we became friends, and during our stay, I made a few friends, a Kenyan student and Egyptian man.

My plan to work in New Zealand did not materialise, and Frank and I came back to South Africa, Cape Town. We remained in touch for a couple of months and since then I never met Frank again.

*   *   *

Going back to John after he was released from the prison, Andrea never got to see him, and he moved to streets of Cape Town selling drugs and doing different kinds of crimes.

He has lost contact with his mother and his sister finally John was arrested for a serious crime of murder, and he was sentenced for twelve years of full Jail term.

In the course of twelve years, he has been transferred to many different Prisons within the region and he becomes a member of a different gang group in side the prison.

While serving at prison, he was badly assaulted, sexually as well as physically and he made several attempts of suicide. The last time he tried by burning himself on fire. Fortunately, he survived all attempts. Nolin was the only one who visited John at the prison from time to time.

Counting the number of years since John was at the prison the year 2003 would be exactly twelve years since his arrest. We had the information, and soon he would be free.

At the end of his jail term, Andrea and myself went to the correctional services. And after we signed all the documents and the necessary formalities, exactly twelve years later John becomes a free man.

It was my first time to see John. At the time of his arrest, I was not even in South Africa. Andrea could not recognise him. He was transformed completely. He becomes old man.

Very skinny, weak and shaky unable to walk properly, but his eyes were very clear and powerful and recognisable, his arms and part of his body is covered with scars of fire burn.

It was the first time more than thirteen years a brother and sister meet and see eye-to-eye and shared emotions. Shortly, we all went together to our new place where we moved recently to Crawford, Athlone.

For couple of weeks he was very polite and a humble person, but that did not last long, he began to behave differently aggressiveness, rudeness and disrespectful, above all he does not control his anger, just like his sister.

It may be understandable the way of life at prison always defensive vocal and aggressive, quit different from the outside world in many ways. I would assume he might require more time to adjust than the time he spent at prison.

The departments of correctional services usually pay a visit to our house for observations, but John usually was not available and it become increasingly hard to persuade John to behave as a normal person. He has learnt many bad things at prison.

John, while he was at prison, has changed his religion, he become a Muslim and gave himself a new name, Ishmael Adams and one of his kidneys has been removed due to infection, on top of that he contracted a TB and many problems at prison.

One week later, he disappeared, and shortly after mid-night, the police phoned confirming the arrest of Ishmael. He was red-handed after he broke in to the house for stealing.

*   *   *

Fernando and John were not close brothers, there is no affections or bond between them, there was no good environment or space of time to grow up together and share emotions.

Fernando has never visited his brother John, while he was languishing at prison for long-term sentence. Fernando by him self has been in prison for numerous occasions for various crimes.

Even after the release of Johan, Fernando did not bother or exited to see his only brother John. It took them more than two years before the two brothers see eye to eye.

Fernando was a member of one of the big gang group in Cape Town area. Lately, he realised that crime does not pay and he becomes tired of the prisons and criminal activities.

Desperately he wanted to get rid of the gang life. He wants to lead a normal life. It was not easy and very risky to get out of the gang group, but there was a woman behind the new idea and change of mindset.

Tanya, a great woman, loved him so much. She was determined to bring about changes in his life, restore his dignity, value, and worthiness for himself and the family.

She took control and in charge of his life in a positive direction for the future of both. For the first time in his life, he begins to discover what normal life is all about. He then follows her advice and guidance.

It was not easy to break away from the gang group. 'It has its own risks and consequences', but he had to make a choice and move on for his morality and well-being. We were fully behind the new idea and gave them all the support they need.

Later that week, he made his own conscious decision, and a couple of days later, they left to an undisclosed area far from Cape Town for their own safety for better future.

Two years later, they had two beautiful boys, and Fernando turned out to be a very happy and responsible father. The last time when I met them, they both were working and doing very well. He was twenty-seven years old.

*   *   *

Nolin was working for a couple of years in a beautiful town of Hermanus, just less than ten miles away from Houston. Her employer is a wealthy and famous old lady, who lived in the outskirts of Hermanus beneath the mountain.

Nolin was getting older; she could not manage to sustain her levels of strength. Later she quit her job. The following year, she was, provided with a small house among other low-income people who applied for subsidy houses in Houston area. She is now fifty-seven and lives on her pension.

The most significant character of Nolin was she loves all her children unconditionally. No matter how difficult and obscure they are, she never gave up on them; she defended them vigorously.

As life went on, I was working on and off in different companies, but I did stay long without a job. Due to the circumstances, I had to be on the job anyway.

Although my profession was that of a diesel mechanic, I took on other unrelated jobs, whenever and wherever jobs were available. However, both of us had to work for long hours in order to survive in Cape Town.

I am of Ethiopian origin. It took me more than three years to obtain a South African identity, and since the middle of 1998, I am a South African citizen.

For a foreigner like me, legal recognition by the government is very important, but that was not enough. Some of the workers including the officials were not willing to accommodate, especially when the immigrant happens to be a black person.

Xenophobia and racism are the biggest challenges in South Africa, which many of us had to face from time to time as an obstacle to rent a house, to find a job, or for promotions.

We may have been discriminated because of our race, colour, and gender. Commonly we have shared painful experiences like many black South Africans; however, when it comes to xenophobia, most people raise against foreigners, killing them and destroying their property.

There are many highly qualified refugees, who survived by selling goods on the street corners, instead of practicing their profession which could benefit both the refugees and the society.

Through my experience in my work place or anywhere else there is always a distinction, and no matter how much honest and hard working one can be, it is very unlikely to be accounted or recognised.

Always regarded as an outsider, an unknown person, alien, it is depressing. I am referring mainly to the black refugees who came from different parts of Africa.

There are people, very few, who are very kind and understanding, accepted me as who I am at my work and in my community. There are genuine and real people who respect and value the dignity of others.

Being ethical or tolerant to other people may cost absolutely nothing, but it has a big effect or impression for those who were deprived. South Africa by itself is a nation racially divided. It probably takes many years to bring the nation together.

In my life, I passed through numerous challenges of different nature. And it also helped me to see through new problems, which I had no experience previously, without panicking.

I believed, life has its pattern—anger, frustration, depression or different kinds of emotions. I usually allow it to pass through me, hoping nothing would remain unchanged.

*   *   *

Andrea was dreaming about writing her book, her life story, the story about her past, but one of the standing blocks in her way was her emotions. She could remember as far as she was four years old.

She wants to start from the beginning. However, after writing a few sentences suddenly she stops writing and start crying. There are many bad things that happened in her life.

Several times, I insisted she should get rid of all the toxins out of her mind but curiosity and uncertainty, fear of rejection and humiliation, fear of the families of the perpetrators kept her away from writing or telling her side of the story to anyone.

From the year 1998, Andrea and I were moving from place to place in search of better accommodation, but finally we have settled in Crawford area for the last nine years.

*   *   *

Most of the Ethiopians who I met here in Cape Town have gone to different parts of the world, through the sponsorships of churches and other means many of them repatriated to Canada and Europe.

Since they left, I have no contact as they scattered in different parts of the world, but there are few Ethiopians who live in Cape Town self-employed, which I do not have close relationship.

Some time ago, I travelled to Johannesburg, and I went to the family house of Mrs Dory Coli, at Hillbrow area, and for two weeks, I stayed with them for some reason. I had a special bond with the family,

Couple of years later, I went to visit again. This time I was not lucky. She has moved to Soweto with her family after her husband has passed away of long illness.

Since I left Ethiopia in 1991, I never got the chance to see my family, except a few letters, which I received while I was in Nairobi, Kenya. It was from Munir my nephew, a teenage boy, a high school student at the time.

Lately, I spend many sleepless nights thinking about my family, colleagues, and my country. Often I talked to Ann seeking for comfort. And constantly I have been occupied with the thought of going back to my origin, to my country.

Most of all, I need to go back to Assossa then to the remotest place, Jarso, the place where my story begins primarily the reason, why I am here today.

We may be far away thousands of miles apart, but we always have contact through our spirit in a distance and there is always hope, and I am driven by this hope to re-unite with the past, with my colleagues.

My main task would be to go back to the remote Jarso, to the forest to make an assessment, to find out how and why it happened in a clear mind. I think that is where I should begin to look for answers.

For the last half century there has never been peace in Ethiopia, change in government, fighting for independent, different political factions and tribal conflicts, hunger, draught so on and so on . . .

There are millions who were affected like myself due to the political unrest, finding their ways to different parts of the world. Many more have been killed even before they get to the next destination.

When I thought about Jarso, I felt uneasiness and discomfort, considering the risk in the journey and the security problems in Ethiopia, as always the country with a political turbulence.

*   *   *

Andrea has just celebrated her fortieth birthday surrounded by families and close friends; she is naturally gifted, likeable, very warm, honest, truthful, and easily excited.

It was the year 2006. Andrea has deeply involved in her religion practice, and she has a regular contact with the pastors and the church leaders. She spends more time on her Christian faith than anything else.

Lately she has been under pressure that she should get a Christian partner rather than a Muslim one like myself, which I was not aware of and she has never told me, but I become very suspicious.

She start by crying, 'I am sorry, I did not want to hurt your feeling, but we cannot continue like this, you are a Muslim and I am a Christian if you still refused to be a Christian we cannot live together'.

That was what I was expecting to hear, I was not surprised considering the circumstances she was in, she was sad as much as I was she has decided to put the religion before me as the obligation.

Couple of times, I was requested by the leaders to attend the church and to Accept Christianity, but I made it clear for everyone, I was unshaken and firm in my believe Islam.

On July 2006, we've divorced for the last time, but we had a commitment to stay in touch for the sake of our son. It was not easy to break away the emotional bond, which we have developed since '95.

*   *   *

The suffering and the challenges which I face over the years, gave me Internal strength. Whenever I faced even tougher problems, I make myself calm down for clear assessment. I usually measure up the new problems against the previous challenges I went through, as a benchmark.

I grew up as any African boy, did not know much about the world. I learnt from life in hard way. Whenever I get problems in any form, I usually step out and see it differently.

Sometimes the smaller problems, which are considered, might turn out to be a solution for the bigger problem, which comes afterwards, which may not be seen at the time.

Over the years I have learnt from life it self, to convert negative thinking to a positive energy, I believe the complex problems and the suffering I went through helped me to discover myself.

In every thing I do, I always tried to be open, direct, honest and truthful. Being honest has its consequences, however truthfulness stimulate more energy and satisfaction to our soul.

BACK TO THE START WHERE IT BEGAN

March 2007. It was time to wrap up, time to go back. It seemed to be the end of my long journey. I started that journey not intending to have any adventure or fun. I was pushed into it by the circumstances.

When I thought about going back, it made me nervous. For the last seventeen years, I never had any contact with my family or my colleagues back in Ethiopia. Since the day I heard the death of my sister Sahara, while I was in Kenya, it made me nervous to think about the rest of my family.

Nevertheless, I had to make a move to break the silence. First, I went to Johannesburg. When I got there, I started to feel one step closer to the old memories. The thought of my family, my country, and my colleagues began to resurface in my mind.

On my arrival to Johannesburg, I went to the area called Mayfair, a few miles away from Johannesburg's central region where many Ethiopians worked and lived. It was where I could get adequate information about Ethiopia.

The next day I met a person. I never expected to see him, not in my wildest dreams. Mr Isaac, sick and depressed, survived by selling goods deep in the rural areas, far from the city of Johannesburg.

Mr Isaac was a successful businessperson in Kenya, Nairobi. I worked for him thirteen years ago. He came to South Africa at the mid of 2005, after he lost everything he owned back in Nairobi, Kenya.

I would imagine it would be very hard to gain his confidence and status back to what it was. He realised he was getting old and sick and needed to change the way he behaved however. I made myself available for anything he may have required.

Two days later, I met an old friend of mine who lived in Johannesburg, a person by the name of Emanuel. Through him, I met someone who was looking for me. The new guy had an old photograph of mine.

He had been sent to look for me from home from my family back in Ethiopia. My sister Sittina and her children, who had grown up, needed to know desperately if I was still alive or dead.

That was the big breakthrough. The new guy provided me with the contact numbers. With that I made my first call nervously to one of my nephews in Addis by the name of Amir.

Dr Amir, when I left Ethiopia, was a young boy in the eighth grade. Since then he had completed his studies and become a medical doctor, specialised in gynaecology.

When I talked to him, we both burst into tears. I was extremely emotional. He sounded nervous, and he was not sure if it was really me, who he was talking to at the other end.

After the identification process, he told me I should not contact my sister Sittina, until he notifies her about me. I understood how much the family had suffered from my being lost for so many years.

Couple of days later I got a call from a hotel situated at the outskirts of Johannesburg airport. The young man introduced himself as Tibebu.

Tibebu was the pilot in the Ethiopian Airways and a dear friend of Amir. He wanted to see me in his hotel as a matter of urgency, as he was flying the next morning back to Addis.

On his way to Johannesburg, he was sent by my family to capture my image on the video tape he carried, as a confirmation. I spent a couple of hours with him. From that moment I became nervous.

*   *   *

On 9 February 2008, I flew from Johannesburg to Addis, Ethiopia. The next day, on my arrival at the airport, my heart started pounding faster and faster. I knew my families and friends would be at the airport.

As I found my way out from the airport, there were many peoples. I hardly recognised any of them. Physically, they had grown up and changed and some of them become older.

I was so confused, but I noticed someone standing between my family members—the young pilot Tibebu, who I met at the Johannesburg hotel. Through him I was able to identify my people one by one.

Shortly after that, I was taken to a house that belonged to the family not far from the airport. I spent the night surrounded by families and friends. It was one of the happiest moments in my life.

The next morning we drove about 150 miles to my birthplace, Dilla, where Sittina and the rest of our family lived. On our arrival, I met many people of the surrounding areas.

I was amazed the little ones had grown up. Some of them had become academicians, engineers, high school teachers, and doctors.

I was deeply saddened that my younger brother Saeed who has passed away. and some of my close relatives and friends have passed away as far as more than ten years ago, which Iwas not aware at the time.However, I was very proud of the younger kids for their achievements while I was in a foreign country.

Sittina is my older sister, strong and beautiful kind hearted as she used to be. She cried and mourned for many years. Even when most people speculated I was dead, she was one of the few who believed I was alive.

One week later, Amir went back to his job, which is far from Dilla at the hospital located in the small town called Gimbi in Jarso.

It was my intention long before I came to my country to go to Jarso and all those places, and it would be a good opportunity to have him around when I go to those places in the near future.

I had a good rest with my family in Dilla. Two months later, I need to go to Addis to meet my colleagues who were with me previously at the Fashim detention camp in Sudan.

After the incident at 'Sirba 1' Jarso, the AMSC has been liquidated and integrated to smaller private-owned enterprises. Most of the workers have been re-trenched, and a few of them passed away.

I met my old friend, the administrative head, Zewde, who came to collect us from the town of Nekempt on our return from the Fashim camp. I also met a few old employees who remained at the AMSC. My first question to them was this: where are my Jarso colleagues?

I heard the bad news of the deaths of Tolossa and Haile a few years ago. But Gecho was alive although not completely well. Currently he is working for AMSC at one of the branches not far from the capital Addis.

Zewde did not have enough information about the rest of my colleagues—Faisel, Yonnas, Tamiru, and those farmers Assefa, Seido, Tilahun, and Mekonnen the settler.

To get more information, I decided to have contact with my colleagues who may be alive. It was about seventeen years since I left the country and I had no contact with them during all those years. It would be more difficult to acquire information about Fiona and Marry, as they lived in Europe.

After a short stay in Addis, I left for Ghimbi, a small town where Munir works at a hospital. Ghimbi is located on the highway line to the towns of Nedjo Jarso and Assossa.

When I got to Ghimbi, I was told many stories about the settlement areas and the activities of the settlers. There had been a radical transformation. Those tiny villages eventually had become bigger towns.

The settlers had changed, the forest land become large farm areas divided into units flourished with different kinds of crops. No more hunger, no more famine deaths.

The kids who were born at the settlement areas had grown up by seventeen more years. Many shops, schools, clinics, and roads had been built. Different climate, different vibe. I cannot wait to see Megelle, Jarso, and all the settlement areas.

Seventeen years seemed to be a short period of time to change the forest into towns, but they had achieved many of the things they had dreamed about. I think when things get going changes are inevitable.

A week later, Amir organised everything for us to go to Jarso, the starting point of my miserable life. I understood he was very busy with patients all the time.

I did not want to take him off from his duty. He had an important job to do; many sick people needed his assistance. I decided to put aside my personal wish and wait for the appropriate moment.

A few days later, I went back to Addis, and a week later, I made a call to Cape Town to find out about Andrea and my son Noor. During my call, Andrea told me something I never expected. I got the shock of my life.

Andrea broke the bad news: 'Your son Noor had a car accident. His left leg has been broken. He is at the hospital.' My body stopped working and my head started aching. I felt helpless.

I loved my son dearly. I did not sleep. I made numerous calls through the night and the following day to Andrea and close friends who lived in Cape Town, South Africa, but I was not satisfied with the answers I was given—'he will be fine do not worry.'

I told Amir the incident and later to Sittina and the rest of the family. We decided that I would go back to South Africa to see my son as soon as possible.

I was closer to Jarso to complete the big circle however. I had all the information I needed, and it was not my intention to come back to South Africa so quickly, but I loved my son to the extent that I would do anything. I decided to terminate my trip to Jarso for a while.

Just one week after the incident, I flew to South Africa. I met Andrea on my arrival. She explained how and where the incident took place. It was hit and run. She guided me to the hospital specially designed for disabled children for physiotherapy.

When I saw him the first time, the lower part of his leg had been broken into two pieces, and the bones were connected by means of screws drilled across the skin and supported by two steel plates, which were visible from the outside.

My first reaction was one of shock, but soon I realised he had been suffering. He needed my close attention. I had to put aside my emotions and comfort him and be there for him.

He was brave enough to swallow the pains. He had multiple operations on his lower limb. Later, the screws and metal plates have been removed, and three months after the injury, he gradually started walking.

He may require many months before he fully recovered. For now, he attended the hospital once a week for check-ups. I decided to go back to my country with my son Noor. With that hope I was counting the days, until he got better.

*   *   *

Nolin did not approve our divorce. She always wanted me to be her son-in-law. Whenever I made a call to her, she reminded me, 'I should not leave Andrea alone. I should be there for her.' But Andrea and I had a different idea.

Despite his illness, John never gave up using drugs. He remained at home insecure, unreliable, and above all mentally unstable. He lived with his mother Nolin in Houston.

Fernando spent most of his life on the run or in jail, but since Tanya came in to his life, he had been out of crime. Unfortunately, he had been on the wanted list by South African Police for serious crimes he had committed previously.

Tanya, Fernando's girlfriend, lived with Nolin. Unemployed, she raises their two kids. Andrea and I had great respect for Tanya for the commitment and sacrifices she had made to change Fernando's life.

I have heard the death of the old woman, Mrs Gerda, of cancer, and one week later, Mr Bashir of Grassy Park also passed away due to natural illness.

*   *   *

Since I came from Ethiopia, I was so amazed by the character of Andrea. She had completely changed. She made me feel welcome. She was very polite and showed no aggressiveness. We respect our boundaries. Just good friendship and nothing more.

As far as I could remember, it was the first time I and Andrea are sitting face-to-face discussing matters, which affected both of us for long hours with out fighting or yelling, based on mutual understanding.

Everything has its end. I need a closure. I already moved on, but there is always something pulling me back. I have to go back to Jarso with my son Noor where my story began. That would be my focus.

My son needs to know everything I went through, which I kept to myself. I could see clearly even those things that I considered to be insignificant at the time.

I am able to remember and recognise any particular incident which took place during my long journey—the approximate time, the weather, and even the circumstances in which something happened.

When I started writing, it was a battle against myself. Different kinds of emotions. At times it made me cry, angry, sad, embarrassed and depressed, and gave me many sleepless nights. Often I stopped writing and sat thinking for hours.

Gradually in the process I felt free, relieved as if a big burden was taken off my shoulders, which I carried for many years. I felt easiness deep from inside as my writing progressed.

* * *

One Sunday morning in October 2007, I got a call from a person. The man introduced himself, but I could not remember a thing about the person who was talking at the other end.

It took me a while before I recognised the voice. I needed to go back seventeen years into my memories in order to understand the young man who I met at Walda refugee camp in Kenya by the name of Meskerem.

The next day when we met, I hardly recognised him. He looked like an old man.
It was my first time I met Meskerem since I left Walda. He had been in South Africa for the last two years, doing business.

During the time of our escape from Walda, Meskerem had been very ill of malaria. We advised him to stay until he got better. One month later, after he recovered, he managed to escape with two of his friends.

After four days in harsh desert, they were caught by the Kenyan security forces and sent back to prison for a couple of months. He remained in Nairobi for more than ten years before he made it to South Africa. Currently he is married and lives in Cape Town.

* * *

Any political group, activist, or organisation that pursues any ideology to gain political power may cause the death of many innocent people. I believe someone has to be responsible or accountable for the brutal killings of innocent men, women, and children.

I have witnessed many killings in Ethiopia. During the war against resistance fighters, many innocent people have been killed, thousands people have lost their property and many more fled the country searching for better life and security.

Recruiting under aged soldiers, the brutal killing and torture by the so-called freedom fighters in the forest have similarities of what the fascist government, has been doing with in the big cities, inflicting pain and suffering for milions for Ethiopians.

My story does not intend to reflect any political message by any means, but some of the things that I have witnessed does not allow me to be silent. The torture and killing of innocent children, men, and women in the name of freedom and democracy does not justify and someone has to be held accountable.

I need to tell the true story to someone who would want to listen, and in the process, drain all the toxins of the past out of my system. I could then feel a positive effect within myself. I extracted some of the facts from my old diary that I have been carrying for many years.

Sometimes I wonder how a single incident could possibly have the power to maneuver the rest of my life in a different direction. Previously, I never had a thought to be in South Africa or anywhere else.

Sometimes things do happen unexpectedly and which is beyond our control. I have learned how to adopt and adjust myself with the new environment wherever I go without wasting time and unconsciously going back to old memories.

Many of the people who knew me closely, including my wife and friends at work, hardly know about me. And I have no idea how they would react once they discover who I really am.

Andrea and I had many similarities, particularly when I think of what we have gone through in life in different parts of the world. I think that was the main ingredient that kept us together.

I do not really have an intimate friend whom I can count on. Some of the people might think I am alone and get bored of life, but the fact is I never get bored of being alone.

I had terrible experiences in the last two decades. It took me to the edge, but I do not know why I need to remember and keep it alive. I do not want to let it go.

In order to write I need to go back and live the past and write the truth that comes out of my mind directly in my own way—when and how it happened from the very beginning.

Personally, I believed it was important for me to indicate the true geographical locations and original names of individuals and places throughout my journey. I have done this from the very beginning, although with the exception of a few names, and among them are two persons who have already passed away.

My wife Andrea needed to know everything I wrote. She needed to know my past and had to find out who I really was. I gave her my script to read it through carefully.

I needed to know her idea about everything I wrote. Moreover, I had to know what she thought of me and particularly how I pursued the story that related to her and the family in general.

In addition, I told her to inform her mother in detail, and I needed to know her reaction regarding the specific story I wrote about her. That is important and a confirmation for my writing.

Couple of weeks later Andrea came back after she completed the reading. She cried before she said, 'It is the truth, and I cannot deny it.'
Her mother had mixed emotions—a sense of confronting the reality and guilt, against her pride and integrity, but deep down a feeling of relief.

*   *   *

I would never forget the signal that gave us hope and the directions that saved our life—the eucalyptus tree. I always have great respect for this tree. I hope Andrea and my son would be able to understand why I was passionate about the eucalyptus.

This tree has a significant meaning deep in my heart. The first time when we discovered it from the top of the mountain, we considered it beyond a tree, a human being.

We consider the Eucalyptus tree as the indicator, our guidance back to civilisation, back to life that was our last green hope, it was a critical moment as we have no direction or energy to move.

Eucalyptus is a tree native to Australia, having aromatic leaves that yield a colourless oily liquid used by pharmaceuticals, for flavoring, and in perfumes. It is valued as timber. This species are among the tallest trees reaching a height of over 300 ft (91 m).

I cannot describe in words how we became excited after we discovered the eucalyptus. That the tree could only be grown by human beings is what makes it different from the rest of the trees in the forest. There is one just opposite to where I live now in Athlone.

*   *   *

In my long journey, I was fortunate to meet many people of different backgrounds and nationalities. I became close with a few of them whom I still have regular contacts with.

I began the long journey from the tiny farm village 'Sirba 1', Jarso, Kenya, and visited Uganda, Sudan, Mozambique Zambia, Malawi Tanzania, Swaziland, South Africa, New Zealand, and Malaysia. I happened to be in many countries, but never intended to have all this adventure.

I think the time has come to go back to my origin, from where it all started, from the beginning, to 'Sirba 1', Jarso, to that jungle forest which is where I should put everything to rest.

The morning of July 1987, was the starting of a critical chain of events maneuvering my life in different directions, I have changed in many ways, it made me see things prospectively, I have learned to be patient and appreciate, most of all never to give up.

I proved to myself that in life there are no hurdles on our way to reaching our dreams. I refused to be restricted by temporary obstacles. No matter how doomed our lives may look, there is always hope which shines afterwards.

The little hope I had never diminished, but it requires a great deal of patient and courage to accomplish, initially I was driven by the ambitions to get to the next stage. This has been my way of life, since two decades ago.

At the time of the incident and after the kidnapping took place, the story was published by newspapers in neighboring countries, Kenya and Yemen, but at the time, it was unknown to us.

Sometimes I browse on the Internet to learn about kidnapping stories, and recently I found a very interesting story with the pictures of Fiona and Marry entitled 'the long walk to freedom'.

I was thrilled and overwhelmed by excitement to find out about the two great women, Fiona and Marry. I have seen the topic with their pictures, but I did not see the documentary. Since then I was motivated to go ahead and publish *Full Circle,* which I had sealed away since 2008.

I would like to thank Andrea, her mother, Nolin, and a half-sister, Joanne, who provided me with many details, and the rest of the family dearly for their moral support, encouragement, and information they provided during my journey, through this small book.

I have a dream—to invite my colleagues of Jarso in the near future for the big journey, from Jarso to Fashim, exactly the same root, through the thick misty forest and difficult terrain of Mountains, a peaceful and enjoyable journey to close the chapter.

Thank you for reading!

True story
(Full Circle)
alimohammed@mail2london.com
Ali Mohammed
(Alimohd)
1988-2008

INDEX